Battleground

CU00649778

FORT EBEN EMAEL

Other guides in the Battleground Europe Series:

Walking the Salient *by* Paul Reed
Ypres - Sanctuary Wood and Hooge *by* Nigel Cave
Ypres - Hill 60 *by* Nigel Cave
Ypres - Messines Ridge *by* Peter Oldham
Ypres - Polygon Wood *by* Nigel Cave
Ypres - Passchendaele *by* Nigel Cave
Ypres - Airfields and Airmen *by* Michael O'Connor
Ypres - St Julien *by* Graham Keech

Walking the Somme *by* Paul Reed
Somme - Gommecourt *by* Nigel Cave
Somme - Serre *by* Jack Horsfall & Nigel Cave
Somme - Beaumont Hamel *by* Nigel Cave
Somme - Thiepval *by* Michael Stedman
Somme - La Boisselle *by* Michael Stedman
Somme - Fricourt *by* Michael Stedman
Somme - Carnoy-Montauban *by* Graham Maddocks
Somme - Pozieres *by* Graham Keech
Somme - Courcelette *by* Paul Reed
Somme - Boom Ravine *by* Trevor Pidgeon
Somme - Mametz Wood *by* Michael Renshaw
Somme - Delville Wood *by* Nigel Cave
Somme - Advance to Victory (North) 1918 *by* Michael Stedman
Somme - Flers *by* Trevor Pidgeon
Somme - Bazentin Ridge *by* Edward Hancock
Somme - Combles *by* Paul Reed
Somme - Beaucourt *by* Michael Renshaw
Somme - Redan Ridge *by* Michael Renshaw
Somme - Hamel *by* Peter Pedersen
Somme - Villers-Bretonneux *by* Peter Pedersen
Somme - Airfields and Airmen *by* Michael O'Connor

Arras - Vimy Ridge *by* Nigel Cave
Arras - Gavrelle *by* Trevor Tasker and Kyle Tallett
Arras - Bullecourt *by* Graham Keech
Arras - Monchy le Preux *by* Colin Fox
Arras - Airfields and Airmen *by* Michael O'Connor

Hindenburg Line *by* Peter Oldham
Hindenburg Line Epehy *by* Bill Mitchinson
Hindenburg Line Riqueval *by* Bill Mitchinson
Hindenburg Line Villers-Plouich *by* Bill Mitchinson
Hindenburg Line - Cambrai RightHook *by* Jack Horsfall & Nigel Cave
Hindenburg Line - Saint Quentin *by* Helen McPhail and Philip Guest
Hindenburg Line -Bourlon Wood *by* Jack Horsfall & Nigel Cave
Cambrai - Airfields and Airmen *by* Michael O'Connor

La Bassée - Neuve Chapelle *by* Geoffrey Bridger
Loos - Hohenzollern Redoubt *by* Andrew Rawson
Loos - Hill 70 *by* Andrew Rawson
Oppy Wood *by* David Bilton
Aubers Ridge *by* Edward Hancock
Fromelles *by* Peter Pedersen
Mons *by* Jack Horsfall and Nigel Cave

Accrington Pals Trail *by* William Turner

In The Footsteps of the Red Baron *by* Michael O'Connor & Norman Franks
Poets at War: Wilfred Owen *by* Helen McPhail and Philip Guest
Poets at War: Edmund Blunden *by* Helen McPhail and Philip Guest

Poets at War: Graves & Sassoon *by* Helen McPhail and Phil
Gallipoli *by* Nigel Steel
Gallipoli - Gully Ravine *by* Stephen Chambers
Gallipoli - Landings at Helles *by* Huw & Jill Rodge
Walking the Italian Front *by* Francis Mackay
Italy - Asiago *by* Francis Mackay

Verdun: Fort Doumont *by* Christina Holstein

Boer War - The Relief of Ladysmith *by* Lewis Childs
Boer War - The Siege of Ladysmith *by* Lewis Childs
Boer War - Kimberley *by* Lewis Childs
Isandlwana *by* Ian Knight and Ian Castle
Rorkes Drift *by* Ian Knight and Ian Castle

Stamford Bridge & Hastings *by* Peter Marren
Wars of the Roses - **Wakefield/ Towton** *by* Philip A. H
Wars of the Roses - **Tewkesbury** *by* Steven Goodch

English Civil War - **Naseby** *by* Martin Marix Evans, Pete
and Michael Westaway
English Civil War - **Marston Moor** *by* David Clarl
War of the Spanish Succession - **Blenheim 1704** *by* James
Napoleonic - **Hougoumont** *by* Julian Paget and Derek Saun
Napoleonic - **Waterloo** *by* Andrew Uffindell and Michael Co

WW2 Fort Eben Emael *by* Tim Saunders
WW2 Dunkirk *by* Patrick Wilson
WW2 Calais *by* Jon Cooksey
WW2 Boulogne *by* Jon Cooksey
WW2 Dieppe *by* Tim Saunders
WW2 Italy – Cassino *by* Ian Blackwell

WW2 Normandy - Pegasus Bridge/Merville Battery *by* Carl S
WW2 Normandy - Utah Beach *by* Carl Shilleto
WW2 Normandy - Omaha Beach *by* Tim Kilvert-Jones
WW2 Normandy - Gold Beach *by* Christopher Dunphie & Garry J
WW2 Normandy - Gold Beach Jig *by* Tim Saunders
WW2 Normandy - Juno Beach *by* Tim Saunders
WW2 Normandy - Sword Beach *by* Tim Kilvert-Jones
WW2 Normandy - Operation Bluecoat *by* Ian Daglish
WW2 Normandy - Operation Goodwood *by* Ian Daglish
WW2 Normandy - Epsom *by* Tim Saunders
WW2 Normandy - Hill 112 *by* Tim Saunders
WW2 Normandy - Mont Pinçon *by* Eric Hunt
WW2 Normandy - Cherbourg *by* Andrew Rawson
WW2 Das Reich – Drive to Normandy *by* Philip Vickers
WW2 Oradour *by* Philip Beck
WW2 Market Garden - Nijmegen *by* Tim Saunders
WW2 Market Garden - Hell's Highway *by* Tim Saunders
WW2 Market Garden - Arnhem, Oosterbeek *by* Frank Stee
WW2 Market Garden - Arnhem, The Bridge *by* Frank Stee
WW2 Market Garden - The Island *by* Tim Saunders
WW2 Battle of the Bulge - St Vith *by* Michael Tolhurst
WW2 Battle of the Bulge - Bastogne *by* Michael Tolhurst
WW2 Rhine Crossing US *by* Andrew Rawson
WW2 Rhine Crossing British/Canadian *by* Tim Saunders
WW2 Channel Islands *by* George Forty
WW2 Walcheren *by* Andrew Rawson
WW2 Remagen Bridge *by* Andrew Rawson

With the continued expansion of the Battleground series a **Battleground Series Club** has been formed to benefit the reader. The purpose of the Club is to keep members informed of new titles and to offer many other reader-benefits. Membership is free and by registering an interest you can help us predict print runs and thus assist us in maintaining the quality and prices at their present levels.

Please call the office 01226 734555, or send your name and address along with a request for more information to:

Battleground Series Club Pen & Sword Books Ltd,
47 Church Street, Barnsley, South Yorkshire S70 2AS

Battleground Europe

FORT EBEN EMAEL

Tim Saunders

Pen & Sword
MILITARY

This book is dedicated to my wife Kate with love.

First published in Great Britain in 2005 by
Pen & Sword Military
an imprint of
Pen & Sword Books Ltd
47 Church Street
Barnsley
South Yorkshire
S70 2AS

ISBN 1 84415 255 3

A CIP catalogue record for this book is
available from the British Library.

Typeset in Palatino

Printed and bound in the United Kingdom by CPI

Pen & Sword Books Ltd incorporates the Imprints of Pen & Sword Aviation, Pen
& Sword Maritime, Pen & Sword Military, Wharncliffe Local History, Pen and
Sword Select, Pen and Sword Military Classics and Leo Cooper.
For a complete list of Pen & Sword titles, please contact
Pen & Sword Books Limited
47 Church Street, Barnsley, South Yorkshire, S70 2AS, England
E-mail: enquiries@pen-and-sword.co.uk
Website: www.pen-and-sword.co.uk

CONTENTS

Acknowledgements 6

Introduction 7

Chapter 1 THE NEED FOR EBEN EMAEL 9

Chapter 2 FORT EBEN EMAEL 19

Chapter 3 GERMAN AIRBORNE AND SPECIAL FORCES 55

Chapter 4 GERMAN PLANS FOR INVASION OF THE WEST 67

Chapter 5 THE FLY IN 85

Chapter 6 THE ASSAULT 93

Chapter 7 HOLDING THEIR GAINS 137

Chapter 8 THE ADVANCE TO THE BRIDGES 153

Chapter 9 THE SECOND DAY 181

Chapter 10 THE AIR ATTACKS ON THE BRIDGES 193

Chapter 11 TOUR OF THE FORT AND BRIDGES 202

            INDEX 208

A *fallschirmjäger* belonging to *Sturmabteilung* Koch during the assault on the Albert Canal bridges.

ACKNOWLEDGEMENTS

My principal acknowledgement is to the outstanding English speaking guides who have conducted me around Fort Eben Emael on numerous occasions over the years and who have answered my many detailed questions. In the early days of my interest in the fort, the guides were invariably Belgian Army soldiers but now serving and ex-members still work at the fort in a voluntary capacity. They provide a soldier's insight that is often missing from written accounts and I unreservedly thank them for sharing their knowledge.

Eben Emael is still Belgian military property and has recently become one of three military memorial sites but the fort is what it is today, thanks to the Friends of Eben Emael (asbl). Their dedication, enthusiasm and work to restore the fort gives it an exciting future; their work in opening galleries and producing displays for visitors is a fine example to those of us who have an interest in twentieth century military history. The fort holds working weekends, when the Friends appeal for volunteers to help restore parts of the defences. In recent years members of the British Parachute Regiment have worked on the fort which all airborne soldiers see as an important part of their collective heritage. If a weekend's hard labour is not to taste, perhaps a donation or even sponsorship could be considered.

I would also like to thank researchers in Belgium, Germany and the United States who have located original reports, maps and photographs in their respective national archives on my behalf and to Liz Fox of Bruge, who did much of the detailed translation when my schoolboy French failed me. I would also like to thank individuals and public bodies that supplied some of the more interesting German photographs of the fort. Finally, I would like to acknowledge the work of fellow soldier Thomas Mouat, whose work on Belgian fortresses, Eben Emael and the issue of the hollow charges in particular, has been a constant 'reality check' on 'history and legend' exemplified by over inflated claims made in some accounts.

INTRODUCTION

'Germany's whole future is in the air and it is by air power that we are going to recapture the German Empire. To accomplish this we will do three things. First, we will teach gliding as a sport to our young men. Then we will build up commercial flying. Finally, we will create the skeleton of a military air force. When the time comes, we will put all three together – and the German Empire will be reborn.'

Reichmarshall Herman Göring

Fort Eben Emael, reputedly one of the most expensive and powerful defensive structures ever built, stands barring the way into the heart of Belgium, on the route that Hitler's Generals originally planned to take in 1939. However, the German main effort was transferred to the Ardennes, south of the 'Maastricht Gateway' which was covered by the fort. Nonetheless, the German attack, via Eben Emael, into central Belgium was important, as it would widen the frontage of the attack, obscure the German main effort from the Allies, attract and fix in battle a significant proportion of the Belgian, British and French Armies. In May 1940, the fort had to be taken even though the plan had changed.

The Germans, in the person of Adolf Hitler himself, saw the solution to neutralising the fort's offensive capability and the reduction of the defences. He looked to new military technologies to solve the problem but, it can also be argued that the fall of Eben Emael was a failure to fully apply modern technology. However, no matter how powerful the technology, it was and still is, the soldier who ultimately decides the outcome of a battle. Training, effective command and communication and, above all, morale, in all its facets, still play a predominant part.

I should point out that as most visitors start a tour of Eben Emael inside the fort, times used for key events throughout this book are Belgian time, which was one hour earlier than German time. These are also the timings that will be quoted when visiting the fort. However, it is apparent from the sources that many events during 10 and 11 May 1940 have a variety of times attributed to them. In cross referencing sources, I have tended to err in favour of Belgian records, as their command posts had the facility to log events and times, whereas the Germans noted times of events in their reports written after the battle.

I hope that I have been successful in presenting both the German and the Belgian view of events in a balanced manner that will allow readers to make their own judgements. However, to those soldiers both Belgian and German, who fought on the Albert Canal and at Eben Emael, particularly to those who gave their lives or health during the battle, I remain in awe of their resilience, dedication to duty and their achievements.

Tim Saunders
Warminster 2005

German infantry crossing the Maas under fire from the defending Belgians, May 1940.

Chapter 1

THE NEED FOR EBEN EMAEL

The military art of fixed fortifications is as old as warfare itself. Complex fortifications have been widely used in   the Low Countries of north-eastern France, Belgium and the Netherlands. Here they were positioned to guard cities and key points on the traditional invasion routes from the north German plain into France (and of course *vice versa*), which General de Gaulle described as 'that fatal avenue'.

Sebastien de Vauban.

Fortress design developed over the millennia, as technology produced both successive new threats and construction techniques to counter them. By the middle of the nineteenth century, the earlier works of the great military architects (chief amongst whom were de Vauban and Coehorn) had been undermined by the pattern of warfare in the Age of Reason and by new weapon designs. The French Revolution, massive rifled gun barrels, breach-loading artillery and piercing shells combined to render the seventeenth-century bastions, ravelins, etc. increasingly obsolescent. Most fortresses were redesigned to include a ring of smaller, mainly concrete forts built outside artillery range of the older citadel defences.

After the treaty of 1871, at the end of the Franco/Prussian War, the Belgians witnessed the French and Prussians building a series of fortifications along their new borders, and it was plain to them that both nations nursed a desire to return to the fight. As a result, in 1877 General Henri-Alexis Brialmont (1821 – 1903) set about modernising the Belgian defences, fearful that the new Second German Reich would be forced to attack Belgium in a future conflict in order to avoid the 'impregnable' defences on the Franco/German border. Chief among the new Belgian defences was the ring of forts positioned on a radius of

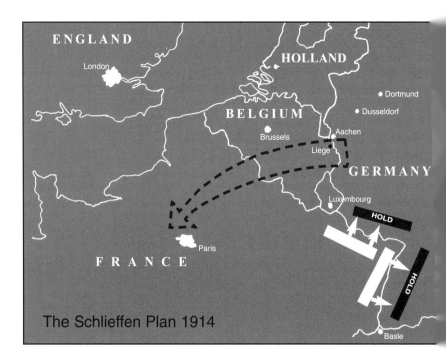

The Schlieffen Plan 1914

approximately 7,000 yards from the older defences of Liege. Sited roughly 4,000 yards apart, the twelve forts were based on a series of armoured cupolas mounting a handful of modern quick-firing artillery pieces. Except for the cupola and galleries that provided covered positions from which infantry could sweep the approaches to the forts with fire, the whole fortress (barracks, magazines and connecting tunnels) was buried underground. Brialmont designed the defences to withstand bombardment by guns of 210 mm calibre. However, as artillery developed, this figure was soon relegated to an arbitrary calibre and defences were not updated to reflect the availability of heavier guns.

Early criticisms of the Brialmont fortifications, however, centred upon human factors:

'The time and difficulty of filing the men out of dark and narrow underground passages and spreading them along the line they are intended to hold, or of getting them under cover again when the besieger's artillery opens fire, may easily be imagined.'

Another commented that:

'Brialmont's military genius had an academic bent, and he forgot that his works were made for human beings; he left out of

> *account a natural function which does not cease during a bombardment – quite the reverse.'*

The rings of modern fortresses built around key Belgian cities, which had been almost completed by the end of the nineteenth century, appeared to compare well with those of the Germans and the French, but in practice they proved to be less than impregnable when subjected to the test of German attack.

Despite the new Belgian fortifications, the Germans were not deterred from attacking Belgium: in fact, the architect of Germany's war plan, Count von Schlieffen, planned to violate Belgium's neutrality. He intended to fix the French in Alsace Lorraine by vigorous attack, while his main body would outflank the French by marching through Belgium. To support this plan, the Germans produced siege artillery to reduce the Belgian fortresses, including the Krupp 420 mm 'Big Bertha' guns. By 1914, Belgium's defences may have been virtually complete, but the fortress lines had some critical deficiencies. One of these was the lack of adequate defences covering the Vise Gap between Maastricht and Liege, for which Brialmont had been denied funding, and he passionately argued that Belgium 'will weep tears of blood for not having built that fort'.

The Austria 12-inch siege mortar, built by Skoda. The type was borrowed by the Germans to reduce the frontier forts in Belgium and France. The gun has been levelled for loading.

Consequently, the Germans were presented with an opportunity to take this route into the heart of the country with relative impunity, as the small Belgian Army's field equipment was obsolete.

In August 1914, faced with artillery of up to twice the calibre that Brialmont had designed the fortresses to withstand, the Belgian defences failed, and the German armies marched on into northern France. The Liege fortresses were the first to feel the might of the German Army under General Ludendorff. The enemy infantry passed through the gaps between the forts of Fleron and Evegnee, as Brialmont, relying on a few quick-firing guns mounted in turrets, failed to produce sufficient volume of fire to halt them. To make matters worse, the Belgian infantry were tied to positions in the forts rather than holding ground between the defensive works, where they could be supported by fire from the quick-firing turrets. In the event some of the forts did not hold out for long, and on 8 August, even before the arrival of the Big Berthas, smaller calibre guns smashed the first of the defences into submission. The lack of adequate steel reinforcing, and a faulty methodology used during pouring the concrete, produced structures that lacked the necessary resilience. In addition, the Belgians had not embraced the simple technology of using layers of sand to absorb the shock of bombardment, which in 1916 allowed fortresses such as Dourmont at Verdun to withstand heavy and sustained bombardment. Consequently, the arrival of the Big Bertha guns on 12 August served only to speed up the reduction of the Liege defences. At 1720 hours, on 18 August, a 420 mm shell penetrated the ammunition magazine of the key Fort of Loncin. The resulting explosion created a large crater in the centre of the fort, which is now a registered war grave for 350 Belgian soldiers. Gun turrets were shattered, sprung out of their mountings and toppled into the crater. The commander of the Liege fortresses was pulled from the rubble of the fort in a shocked state, and promptly surrendered. The remaining forts of Liege fell soon after this disaster. As the main body of the German Army pressed on into northern France, the defences at Namur resisted for only four days, while those of the National Redoubt at Antwerp lasted a little longer, both also succumbing to the German heavy guns.

After the Great War, Belgium initially remained in alliance

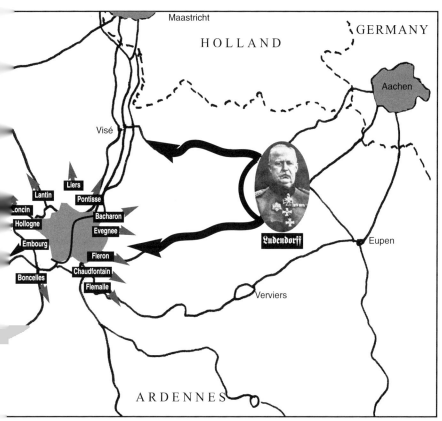

Ludendorff's attack on the Liege fortresses and its ring of defences.

Germans inspecting the wrecked Fort Loncin in August 1914.

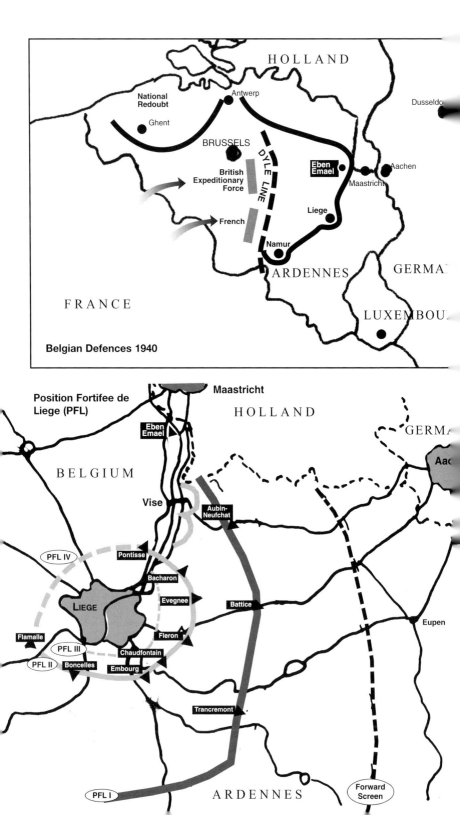

with France. In the late 1920s, however, this alliance proved to be of little value, and the two countries worked on their own defence with minimal effort at coordination. The example of the stout defence of the Antwerp fortresses, the resilience of France's Verdun fortresses, and the Great War victors' belief in the power of defensive systems, led Belgium into a new round of fortress construction. France began building the Maginot Line in 1929 and Belgium started work on reconstructing her own defensive lines, and eventually resumed its policy of defended neutrality in 1936. 'Plucky Belgium' was determined to deter aggression from both the east and west, and to fight to preserve its national integrity.

Between the wars, the new Belgian defences were again based on a system of fortifications and defended lines using natural barriers such as the Meuse and the Albert Canal, along with the older city defences. The Belgian strategy was to delay a potential aggressor (either French or German) in the border

Belgian soldiers erecting barbed wire obstacles on the western bank of the Albert Canal.

Badge – Regiment Fortifiee de Liege.

See map page 14

area in order to buy time for the Belgian Army to mobilise and deploy to its main defensive lines and field positions in the interior of the country. The two lines of particular interest in this book are in the east of the country; the *Position Advancee* and the *Position de Couverture*. The former followed the Belgian German border north from the Ardennes to link up with Liege's outer positions well to the east of the city, and extended further north up the Dutch border to Antwerp. The *Position de Couverture* or Covering Position included the newly enhanced *Position Fortifiee de Liege* (PFL). These two lines joined at a critical point; Eben Emael. Behind these forward lines, which, as already mentioned, were designed to delay the enemy for up to five days, were the main defensive positions based on the River Dyle and the National Redoubt around Antwerp.

By 1940, of the original ring of twelve Liege forts, eight had been redeveloped and new outer works were built. The new outer ring of defences (PFL 1) consisted of four modern forts, including Eben Emael, along with intermediate anti-tank and machine gun casemates, added in order to cover an arc that included the likely German approach to the city from the east. PFL 2 consisted of anti-tank obstacles, six updated forts and sixty casemates mounting machine guns. PFL 3, nearest to the city, covered the main roads into Liege from the east, while PFL 4, to the west of the city and the River Meuse, consisted of two modernised forts and intermediate machine gun casemates. The city's defences were manned by a static formation, the *Regiment de Forteresse de Liege*, which was considered in the Belgian Army to be unglamorous and not the career choice of the active soldier seeking promotion.

Eben Emael was built 'to deter an aggressor from the east from contemplating breaching Belgian neutrality'. However, the deterrent effect was reduced by the size of Eben Emael's largest guns, which were limited to 120 millimetres, a calibre that avoided the accusation of a neutral nation being 'provocatively'

16

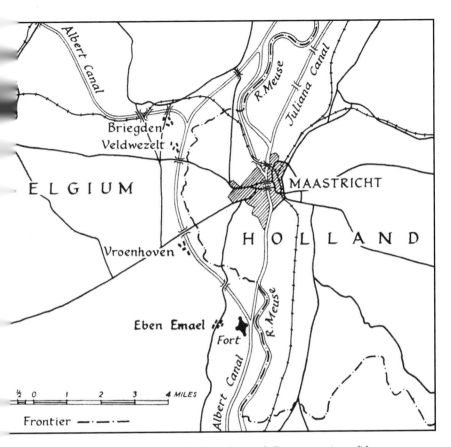

Albert Canal · R.Meuse · Juliana Canal · Briegden · Veldwezelt · ELGIUM · MAASTRICHT · Vroenhoven · HOLLAND · Eben Emael · Fort · R.Meuse · Albert Canal

½ 0 1 2 3 4 MILES

Frontier ——·——·——

able to engage targets on the borders of Germany, just fifteen miles away. Upon the outbreak of hostilities, the fortress, sited to the north of Liege, was designed to cover with long-range fire the previously undefended routes from the east, including the Visé Gap. Closer to the fort, Eben Emael covered the various river and canal bridges. To the north, its guns were sited to engage targets around four defended bridges over the newly-built Albert Canal, which if captured intact would give the Germans access to the Gembloux Gap and routes into central Belgium. To the south of the fort were the bridges over the river and canal at Visé.

The 50-yard-wide Albert Canal had been dug just inside the Dutch/Belgian border, and followed a route west of Maastricht. The canal formed a natural defensive barrier for the Belgians, which was enhanced by pillboxes, infantry positions and barbed-wire defences. With the help of fire support from Eben Emael, this would undoubtedly delay a German advance into

Dutch artillery crew manning border positions near Maastrict, May 1940.

the heart of Belgium. It was envisaged that even if the bridges were captured or the canal line forced by the Germans, Fort Eben Emael would hold out, continuing to delay any elements of the *Wehrmacht* attempting to cross the fort's arcs of fire. This would buy time for the Belgian Field Army to be mobilised and deployed to defensive positions covering the centre of the country.

The Bridge at Veldwezelt

Chapter 2

FORT EBEN EMAEL

On a site that had proved to be a dangerous deficiency in the 1914 Belgian defences, Fort Eben Emael was designed to exploit to the full the natural defensive qualities of a hill between Liege and Maastricht, the River Meuse and the new strategic barrier created by the construction of the Albert Canal. The requirement was for a fortress to complete the updated PFL, which was intended to delay an invader from the east. The fortress that the Belgians decided to build at Eben Emael in 1931 was the centrepiece of the country's defended neutrality, and cost the nation the vast sum of 50 million Belgian francs up to 1936. This amount does not include work carried out between that date and 1940.

The broad plateaux of Saint Peter's Hill or the Caestert Heights overlooking the River Meuse to the east of the villages of Eben and Emael had unrivalled views across the southernmost part of Holland and into Germany. Consequently, the hill had been a defensive position of one type or another

See photo page 204

A pre-war photograph of the *Tranchée de Caster* and the Albert Canal, looking north from Lanaye, with Fort Eben Emael on the left.

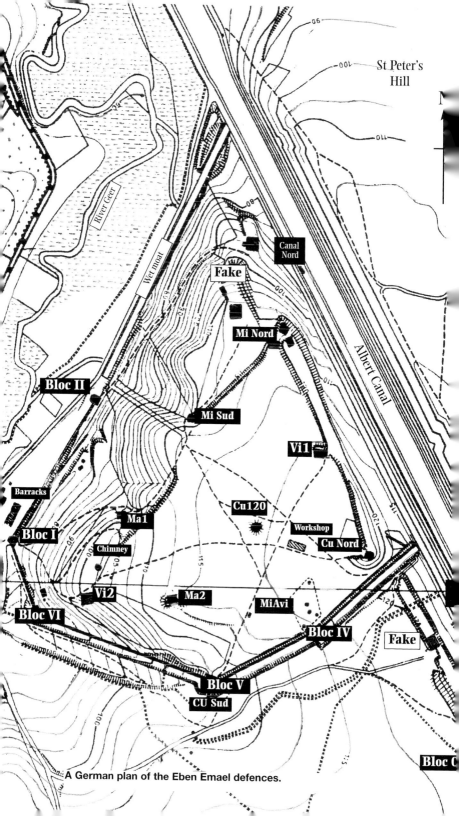

A German plan of the Eben Emael defences.

since fourth-century Roman times, held by a variety of warring tribes and armies. A force operating from Saint Peter's Hill was not only able to observe movement for miles around, but could also control the east-west route via the crossing of the River Meuse at Maastricht, which was all too often used by invading armies.

The creation of the Albert Canal made it possible for the Belgians to build an outstanding modern defensive position at Eben Emael. Planned in 1919, the Albert Canal was a tremendous engineering achievement, particularly the cutting through the marl rock of Saint Peter's Hill *(Tranchee de Caster)*, which linked the Albert Canal with the Sud Willem Canal. This cutting cleaved its way through the hill, creating a near-vertical trench some 65 yards deep, 50 yards wide and 1,300 yards long.

Following the decision to build a state-of-the-art fortress on the naturally strong position at Eben Emael, design work and construction began promptly in 1932, with money being lavished on the project. However, the engineering challenges were such that, controversially, two German contractors worked on external parts of the fortress. Many subsequently argued that as deterrence was a part of Eben Emael's very reason for existence, it was important that the Germans knew how immensely strong the defences were, and it was assumed that they would be duly deterred from taking a route through Maastricht or the Visé Gap.

GENERAL DESCRIPTION

Completed in 1935, the fort, occupying a triangular area some 900 yards long north to south and 800 yards wide at its east-to-west base, was literally built into St Peter's Hill, with only the cupolas, casemates and blockhouses of the various batteries visible above ground. The flanks of the hill were already fortified to the northeast by the Albert Canal in its deep *Tranchee de Caster*, while the slopes of the fort's north-west face were steepened and protected by a wet moat, along with the ability to inundate the Geer Valley. Most of the southern slopes were protected by 12-foot-high walls, a deep moat, barbed wire and anti-tank obstacles. The approaches to the fort were covered by fire from seven defensive blockhouses built into the fort's perimeter, one of which doubled as the main entrance at the foot of the hill. Apart from two machine gun casemates, dummy

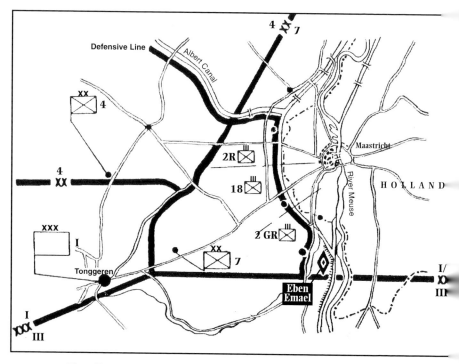

Eben Emael's place in the Belgian defences.

positions, a workshop building and four anti-aircraft machine guns (and not forgetting the garrison football pitch), the upper surface was reserved for artillery casemates and cupolas covering the routes into Belgium to the north and to the south.

Inside Saint Peter's Hill, the fort was on three levels. Off the main passage from the entrance, the Lower Level consisted mainly of barrack and administrative facilities, including messes, a power plant, a well and an infirmary. Up some large staircases, the Intermediate Level, some 120 feet below the surface, contained the magazines and the battery command posts. Following the destruction in August 1914 of Fort Loncin, when its single central magazine was penetrated by a German shell, the Belgian designers elected to provide separate magazines for each artillery position, to avoid possible destruction of the fort by a single event. Access to most of the fort's defensive blockhouses was by stairs down from the Intermediate level, while access to the artillery positions on the Upper Level, for both men and ammunition, was by vertical shafts leading to concrete casemates and cupolas just below the surface.

In addition to the observation posts (OPs) within the fort, there were six artillery OPs outside, connected by telephone cable, sited to cover likely enemy approaches from the east. In concrete blockhouses, two OPs, Caester 1 and 2, were sited across the Albert Canal on the eastern part of Saint Peter's Hill, making the most of the view to the east. Another OP overlooked the Belgian positions surrounding the Kanne Bridge across the Albert Canal (later known to the Germans as Objective *Eisen* or Iron). A fourth OP was sited to engage targets with the fort's artillery in the area of the Vroenhoven Bridge, and another at Briegden had a similar role further north. The sixth OP was located at Loen, south of the fort, from which the area of the Canal and the River bridges west of Visé could be clearly seen. Artillery officers at these OPs were to pass targeting information to Eben Emael's battery command posts, correct the fall of shot onto the target, and then give the order for the guns to 'fire for effect'. Despite the reasonably good coverage by observers, it is thought that Eben Emael's casemated guns could not effectively cover the approaches to the bridges north of the fort, via Maastricht, due to the limited arcs of fire imposed by the height of Saint Peter's Hill.

EBEN EMAEL'S GARRISON

The 1st or 'Offensive Battery' comprised the north-and south-facing artillery casemates and the three gun cupolas, while the 2nd, or 'Defensive Battery', manned the blockhouses surrounding the fort and the various machine guns on the upper surface. These batteries, each of approximately 500 men, were theoretically divided into two identical watches that rotated every seven days. The on-duty watch lived in the underground barracks within the fort, while off-duty watch lived in barracks at the village of Wonk, four miles from the fort. This was a deliberate move to ensure that the off-duty gunners would not be within the target area of a surprise bombing attack on the fort. The downside was, of course, that the full compliment of defenders would take a considerable time to assemble, march to the fort and reinforce the on-duty watch already manning the fort's bunkers and casemates.

The third group consisted of the fort's 200 command, technical and administrative soldiers, who worked routine

Major Jottrand and the officers of Fort Eben Emael photographed after the attack.

hours in and around the fort. They provided the sundry combat support and administrative functions, ranging from medics through signallers to repair technicians. In addition to some more senior soldiers of the other two batteries, a high proportion of the command and admin group had local houses, living with their families in the surrounding villages. Though not operationally desirable, soldiers 'living out' is an inevitable result of long-term manning of a static defensive position.

In theory, the fort's wartime establishment totalled 1,185 men, under the command of a major, but Eben Emael was not a popular or healthy posting, and the prolonged Phoney War meant that on 10 May 1940 the fort was seriously undermanned. Firstly, there were men sick with throat and chest problems attributed to the dusty atmosphere inside the fort. Secondly, the posted strength was down by about 100 gunners, mainly because men whose period of conscription had ended were discharged without replacement: so heavy was the demand for manpower in the Belgian field army, with invasion threatening the country. A part of this deficiency of a hundred men was also because important workers such as farmers and miners were released back into civilian life. Finally, a leave ban had eventually been lifted on 9 May, allowing another hundred men due leave to promptly set off home. With other men absent on compassionate leave, the Garrison was at least 250 men below full operational strength at its crucial moment in history.

It has already been recorded that a posting to the Regiment de Forteresse de Liege was considered to be unglamorous and not the choice of the ambitious soldier. In addition, a static unit was a natural place to post older soldiers and those of a lower physical capacity. However, the coarse filter of the Belgian conscription system ensured that this tendency was mitigated, to some extent, by drafting a cross-section of men to the fort. It should be pointed out that while the fort was not a generally popular posting, particularly among conscripts, a number of the permanent regular-army officers and NCOs had been at the fort for years, some since its first gun positions were commissioned, before construction was completed. While these men clearly knew the fort inside out and exactly how it worked, there have been persistent accusations that most were less than

Inside the casemate and the breech and workings of one of the 75mm guns where the Belgian artillerymen worked to fight off the *fallschirmjäger*.

A Belgian gunner depicted manning one of the fort's radios.

inspirational leaders or even sound commanders.

The state of training among the gun crews was not particularly high. The turnover of conscripts was a perennial problem, and a fixed fortification had a particular problem in firing its armaments, which is essential to complete training. Such was the pressure on the Belgian Artillery School that they had no time to address the training needs of the fortress artillery. Consequently, a significant proportion of the gun crews had not actually fired a live round, and their knowledge was based on theory and limited gunnery drill exercises.

The morale of the Eben Emael Garrison is generally considered to have been low, with the fort being nicknamed 'The Education Centre'. Life as a fortress artilleryman was dull, repetitive and unhealthy, without natural light and with few recreational opportunities. Tension between the Flemish and Walloon soldiers and drunkenness had been reported, but little appears to have been done to address these issues or the overall morale of the Garrison.

The months spent trying to maintain soldiers at a high state of readiness, particularly with the repeated false alarms over the winter of the Phoney War, had had its effect. Inevitably, boredom had set in, corners were being cut to make life easier, and the initial high state of readiness was, in practice, progressively watered down.

Another significant weakness in the garrison was that the soldiers were nearly all artillerymen, and apart from basic drills with the Belgian copy of the Mauser rifle had no training in infantry fighting or tactics. Although this was one aspect of military training that the garrison could have practised on and around the fort, the possibility was ignored. These cumulative circumstances allowed officers and men to sink into a 'fortress mentality'. Consequently, counter-attack plans for Eben Emael relied on the infantry from surrounding divisions being diverted from their primary task of holding the Albert Canal. To make matters worse, there were no direct communications with the infantry element of the divisions tasked with mounting counter attacks, as all messages had to be relayed through the artillery chain of command or Headquarters *Regiment de Forteresse de Liege*. This factor was to have a profound effect on the outcome of the battle.

DETAILED DESCRIPTION
The following paragraphs describe each of the main features of the fort. The Belgian names and abbreviations are used throughout, but where appropriate, the figure in brackets indicates the objective number assigned by the Germans. To save repetition, common features will be described at their most significant occurrence, and on other occasions simply listed in the text.

EXTERNAL
Within the barbed-wire perimeter, just outside the entrance to the fort, were a pair of barrack/admin buildings. These had been kept from the construction phase, as it quickly became apparent that the subterranean life-style for the fort's day-to-day commanders and administrators was unpleasant and not conducive to effective work. In the event of hostilities, it was intended that the crews of the two Upper Level machine gun casemates, Mi Nord and Mi Sud, would move documents into the fort and demolish these buildings. This would ensure that

Machine gun

Searchlight

Anti-tank gun

To the left of the fort's gate at Bloc I are the principal elements of the ground defence. Note that the main armament, a 60 mm anti-tank gun, has a protective jacket around the protruding barrel.

Bloc I and the fort's entrance bear the scars of battle.

Observation Bell

Blockhouses (Bloc) I & II had uninterrupted coverage and allow overlapping arcs of fire across the flat ground around the entrance at the southwest corner of the fort. The approach to the fort in this area was only physically protected by barbed-wire fences and triangular steel dragons-teeth anti-tank obstacles: hence the importance of ensuring a clear field of fire.

THE LOWER LEVEL

180 feet below the grassy upper surface of the fort, the installations of the lower galleries were accessed at the level of Eben Emael village. Two broad categories of features are described in this section: the seven defensive blockhouses (Blocs) of 2nd Battery, and the fort's various internal administrative facilities.

Bloc I (German Objective 3) This massive concrete construction, like the other six 1st Battery defensive positions surrounding the fort, was set into the walls and steep slopes surrounding Saint Peter's Hill. As this blockhouse was also Fort Eben Emael's entrance, it was particularly well armed. Two lieutenants, three corporals and 23 soldiers manned a small headquarters, searchlights behind bullet-proof glass, two machine guns and a pair of 60 mm anti-tank guns covering arcs to the north and west respectively. Guns of 60 mm calibre were large for the 1930s, and as static weapon systems they had heavy barrels, breaches and recuperating systems that gave them greater range than a lighter field piece would have had. In this case, the 60 mm guns of Eben Emael were claimed to be effective against tanks of the day at 3,000 metres. Finally, in common with all the defensive blockhouses, there was a small cast-steel observation 'bell' sited on top of the work.

See map on page 20 for locations

Bloc II (4) Sited 275 yards north of the fort's entrance at Bloc I, this position's arcs of fire covered the Canal Nord (the 'wet moat') and, in the opposite direction, overlapped with Bloc I's coverage of the open approaches to the fort from the village. This blockhouse also mounted two 60 mm anti-tank guns, searchlights for night engagements, and two machine guns. Bloc II also had one of the three sally ports, from which the garrison could counter attack an enemy force, in this case in the area of the entrance.

Each of the blocs had a small steel observation bell so that the crews could observe the approaches to the fort.

Bloc Canal Nord (17) On the eastern face of the fort, in the *Tranchée de Caster*, two blockhouses were sited to cover the 50-yard-wide Albert Canal. Bloc Canal Nord's primary arc of fire for its single anti-tank gun and one machine gun was sited to fire north towards Kanne and the towpath on the bank opposite. A second machine gun was located to fire down the *Tranchée* towards Bloc Canal Sud, to provide mutual support between the two blockhouses. Bloc Canal Nord, along with Canal Sud, and Blocs 01, IV, V and VI, had small armoured escape hatches for the gun crew.

See picture on page 19

Bloc Canal Sud (35) Also sited in the *Tranchée de Caster,* towards the southern end, this blockhouse covered the junction of the Albert and Sud Willem Canals, as well as the Lanaye Locks. It was this area that the single 60 mm gun was mounted to cover, while the pair of machine guns covered arcs to the north and south. The Canal Sud blockhouse no longer exists, as it was demolished when the Belgians widened Albert Canal after the war.

Bloc 01 (34) This blockhouse was about 300 yards beyond the southern extremity of Eben Emael, immediately above the Lanaye Locks. The concrete blockhouse was connected to the fort by stairs and a tunnel from the Intermediate Level, which could be blown up to prevent the enemy entering the fort from this outlying position. It would take some twenty minutes for the crew to march from the barracks on the lower level through the tunnels to their positions, where they would man an anti-tank gun and a pair of machine guns. Their main task was again to engage targets around the locks. However, the most important feature of Bloc 01 was the large artillery OP (Eben 1) sited on the roof of the blockhouse. From this elevated position, the observation officer could look out across the Meuse and its valley to the vital target area of the Visé Gap.

Bloc IV (30) (there was no Bloc III) Sited in the deep anti-tank moat on the southern edge of the fort, Bloc IV was equipped with two anti-tank guns, along with searchlights and machine guns. The approaches to the fort across the farmland to the south were blocked by barbed wire and by heavy steel tetrahedral anti-tank obstacles. Many of these items from the Belgian fortresses eventually found their way onto the beaches

A modern view of the Bloc Canal Nord built into the near vertical face of the widened Albert Canal cutting.

The view across the now overgrown dry anti-tank moat to the south of the fort to Bloc IV. Its weapons were sited to cover the moat which extends to the left and right. Note the prominent observation bell.

of Normandy and the rest of Hitler's Atlantic Wall.

Bloc V (22) This blockhouse was located at the southern extremity of the main fort, covering the anti-tank moat. Bloc IV had an establishment of one Non-Commissioned Officer and 16 men who crewed a single 60 mm and a pair of machine guns. Their task was to cover the southern and south-eastern approaches to the fort.

Bloc VI (6) Completing the ring of largely mutually-supporting defensive blockhouses surrounding the lower level of the fort, Bloc VI contained a pair of 60 mm guns, a single machine gun

Bloc VI viewed from the area of the entrance.

and a searchlight. It too was able to engage targets on the vulnerable approaches to the fort's entrance.

LOWER LEVEL – THE INTERNAL FEATURES

Entering Fort Eben Emael at the Lower Level, some 180 feet below the upper surface of the fort, the visitor enters the garrison's living and administrative area. The access tunnel or passage is wide, as it was through this entrance that, once construction was completed, all material, ammunition and stores of all kinds had to be brought into the fort.

Bloc 1 (3) – Internal A pair of 14-foot-high iron-railing gates opened into the entrance chamber and controlled day-to-day access to the fort. Here the main internal entrance defences began with a 15-foot sliding wooden drawbridge over a large pit, 10 feet deep, which barred the way into the fort's interior. As the fort was designed to operate in a gas/chemical environment, a decontamination room opened off the entrance, where men whose clothing and equipment had been exposed to persistent substances such as mustard gas would be cleaned down, or contaminated items would be abandoned. Opposite the Decontamination Room is the heavy armoured steel door to Bloc 1 defensive positions and the guardroom.

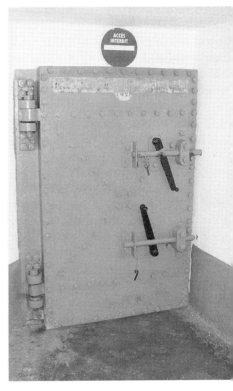

A heavy armoured doorway also bars the main entrance to the tunnels of the fort's interior. As well as being able to resist traditional explosive charges and enemy fire, the door was designed to seal the fort against attack with gas. It should be noted that there was no protective wall or bend in the entrance tunnel to protect the

The heavy armoured steel door to Bloc I is just inside the fort's entrance.

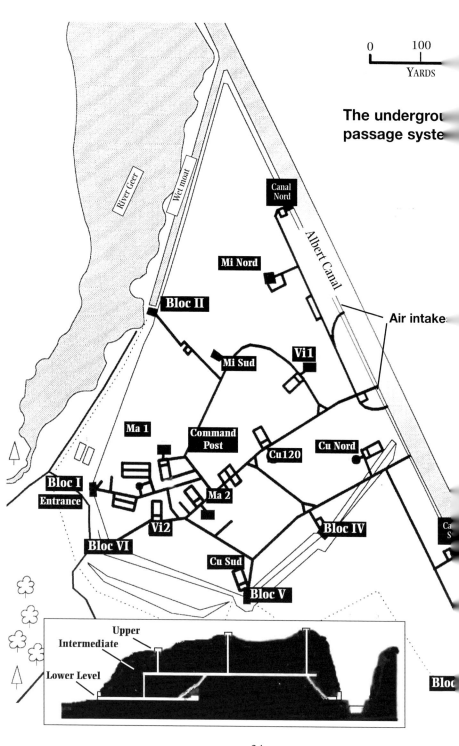

The undergrou[nd]
passage syste[m]

0   100
YARDS

River Geer

Wet moat

Canal Nord

Albert Canal

Mi Nord

Air intake

Bloc II

Mi Sud

Vi1

Ma 1

Command Post

Cu120

Cu Nord

Bloc I
Entrance

Ma 2

Bloc IV

Ca S

Vi2

Bloc VI

Cu Sud

Bloc V

Upper

Intermediate

Lower Level

Blo[c]

34

door from direct fire from the exterior. This has been criticised as a general design fault in Brialmont fortifications. The entrance hall was, however, covered by a machine gun mounted in an embrasure to the left of the door.

Inside the door, a tunnel of just under 200 yards in length, with a 25-degree light bend, runs into the heart of Saint Peter's Hill. The following facilities are located along this tunnel.

Armourers Workshops Weapons including the fortress's guns and small arms would need repair and servicing both in peace time and during war. Therefore, the Eben Emael had a complement of armourers on its administrative staff, who worked within the defended confines of the fort.

The Ablutions The fort's complement of lavatories, washrooms and shower cubicles for the use of the garrison were located off the main corridor. The ablutions are still in use by the fort's staff and visitors.

The main corridor from the entrance photographed in the area of the ablutions.

The Cells Located beyond the bend were the fort's cells. In common with virtually all static military locations, Fort Eben Emael had its own cell block: with a garrison of nearly 1200 men, there would inevitably be disciplinary incidents resulting in soldiers being sentenced to periods of military detention. In time of hostilities, the cells could also be used to hold a limited number of prisoners of war.

Electrical Generation To ensure that the fort was independent of external utilities, Eben Emael had its own power plant of six 175-horsepower (140 KVA) diesel engines. As well as lighting the tunnels and rooms, these provided electricity to operate various armament and ammunition-handling mechanisms within the fort. Power was distributed from a series of transformers and switches from the adjoining chamber, and the water used to cool the engines was recycled to raise the temperature in the barrack area from its natural year-round 11 degrees Celsius to a more comfortable living temperature. Despite the attempts at heating, however, there were parts of the

One of the fort's generators.

fortress that remained stubbornly cold. The showers in the ablution block also used the heated water. Built into the rock nearby were large fuel tanks, capable of meeting the generators' needs in both peace and war for a protracted period. Finally, a large chimney vented the fumes through a concrete casemate on the upper surface of the fort.

Only one of the original six generating engines is still in place and working. The Germans removed the other five, which had been damaged by the Belgian garrison before the surrender, for repair and use in the Atlantic Wall. Of the five generators, four have now been returned, and volunteers are working to fully restore them and use their power around the fort.

Kitchen Also in this area of the fort are the kitchen (now the cafeteria) and larder stores, essential both in peace and war. Duty soldiers collected their meals from the kitchen and served the food and drink on the tables in their barrack rooms.

Stores No military unit would be complete without its stores and storemen. As a static unit, the range of stores held by Eben Emael was not great, but even so, the fort's quartermaster was required to hold everything, from uniform items, through consumable items such as oil, to spare parts for the guns.

Fort Commander's Office Prior to the German attack, Major Jean Jottrand carried out most of his administrative functions in the wooden buildings at the entrance, but once the attack began, he performed most of his command functions from this suite of

Major Jottrand in his office on the lower level.

Kit inspection in one of the barrack rooms.

The Officers' Mess dining room.

offices rather than the battery command posts on the Intermediate Level.

It was in his office, on 11 May 1940, following a council of war with his officers and warrant officers, and an attempt to stiffen the morale of his men during which he had been heckled, that Major Jottrand eventually made his decision to surrender the fort.

Barracks Almost 200 yards from the entrance is the main tunnel intersection or crossroads. A right turn leads to the barrack accommodation area. Through doors carved in the right-hand wall, there are 24 soldiers' barrack rooms, each equipped with beds for up to 20 men. The barrack furniture was spartan: just tables, chairs and personal equipment lockers for each man. On the opposite side of the corridor were the officers' rooms, either single for the more senior officers or shared for the lieutenants, etc. Nearby were the officers' mess rooms, where the officers of the duty-watch would dine together and relax.

Also in the barrack area were small-arms and reserve-ammunition magazines.

Stairs and Lift At the end of the barrack accommodation spur, beyond the steel doors, are the Grand Staircase and the lifts up to the Intermediate Level. Also in this area is a part of the fort's air filtration system, essential to a barrack area accommodating over 500 men at any one time.

Infirmary In a spur leading from the opposite side of the main tunnel intersection is the fort's infirmary. In line with Eben Emael's status as a combat unit, this was quite a large facility, containing a pre-op room, an operating theatre, a dental surgery and a 7-bed ward.

Pump Room The fort had its own water supply, with water being drawn from a borehole located in a room almost at the centre of the fort, and moved by electric pump to storage in tanks above this chamber.

Stairs The fort's Lower and Intermediate Levels could be isolated in the event of gas attack or enemy penetration of the fortress by a double airlock set of heavy doors, which originally

Steel airlock doors and stairs beyond.

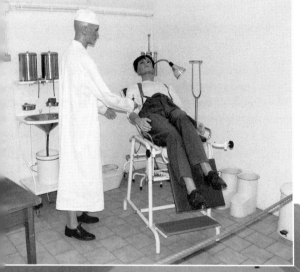

Mannequins occupy the dental surgery and the infirmary's wards.

Opposite: The smaller of the two staircases leading up to the Intermediate Level.

had rubber seals. The stairs rise sixty feet to the Intermediate Level.

The Marl Galleries Surrounding the chambers of the lower level, these narrow, unlined tunnels were rough hewn from the Marl rock and were used to vent foul air from the barrack area of the fortress.

THE INTERMEDIATE LEVEL

This level is a labyrinth of some three miles of tunnel. Such was the complexity of the Intermediate Level that even the garrison needed signs at key junctions to help them navigate from one position to another. Access to all the fighting blocs, casemates and cupolas, the outlying OPs and Bloc I, are from this level. Stairs down from the tunnels of the Intermediate Level give access to the Battery 2's defensive blockhouses, while Battery 1's offensive casemates and cupolas were reached by spiral stairs up the hundred feet to the surface.

See map on page 34

Command Post (CP) Complex The fort had been under operational command of I Army Corps since December 1939, but its guns were tasked to fire across various formation boundaries. The Command Post complex was both physically and figuratively the heart of the fort, and its arrange-ments reflected the command rela-tionships with the other forts of the PFL and formations deployed within range of the Eben Emael guns. The fort's main internal communication system was telephone, backed up by an incomplete intercom system from the battery command posts direct to their respective casemates. External communications were mainly land line, but the fort had three radios.

An officer in one of the fort's command posts.

There were four separate com-mand posts. The principal CP was Major Jottrand's operational Head-quarters; of the remaining three, one controlled the three cupolas of Battery 1's, the second, the same Battery's Visé and Maastrict case-mates, and the third controlled Battery 2's defensive Blocs. Each CP maintained radio and telephone communications reflecting their differing tasks.

The four casemates were allocated to the following regiments:

See map on page 22

Visé 1 (26)	Visé 2 (9)	Maastricht 1(12) & 2 (18
2 Grenadier Regt	2 Rifle Regt	18 Infantry Regt

Details of Battery 1's individual positions will be covered below, but each group of guns was primarily assigned to support one of the surrounding formations, principally of I Corps. However, III Corps, to the south, could call on fire from Eben Emael via *Regiment de Forteresse de Liege,* which was a slow

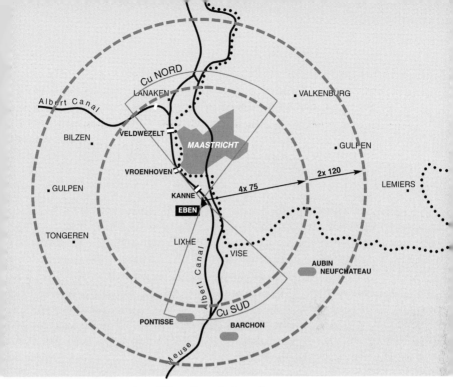

The ranges and arcs of fire of Eben Emael's batteries.

process. The twin 120 mm cupola came under operational command of I Corps's artillery commander, the two twin 75 mm cupolas (Cu Sud and Cu Nord) were given fire orders by 7th Division, and the Visé and Maastricht casemates by infantry regiments that were holding the canal/river line. These affiliations to field formations rather than the PFL reflected Eben Emael's location at the very northern end of the Liege defences, covering some difficult defensive problems caused by the location of the Dutch, Belgian and German borders.

Telephone Exchange The key part of the manual telephone system was also in this area. However, the system did not work particularly well, and the utility of the network was reduced as a number of phones that should have been in the fort were being used at a Belgian Army rifle range some distance away.

Ammunition Magazines There were seven sets of magazine chambers, one set per artillery casemate or cupola. They were located in the Intermediate Level for storing cartridge cases and shells. One hundred and twenty feet below the surface with several protective steel doors, the individual magazines were far less vulnerable than the central magazine that had destroyed Fort Loncin in 1914. Ammunition was loaded into special metal, flash-proof, trolleys in the magazines and wheeled out to the ammunition hoists. The two types of cartridge trolleys contained forty-two 75 mm rounds and fourteen 120 mm rounds respectively.

Ammunition Hoists and Stairs The magazines were located opposite the vertical shafts rising 100 to 120 feet up to the casemates and cupolas. In the centre of the shafts were a pair of ammunition hoists that took the ammunition trolleys up to the casemate. Around the hoists were staircases that provided the only access to the casemates above. The landing plates of the

stairs could be lifted in order to lower or haul up large or heavy items such as gun barrels.

At the foot of the hoist, the 'airlocks' between two sets of doors had slots that were designed to take steel beams and to be packed with sandbags to effectively seal off the casemate from the rest of the fort, if the enemy had broken into the chamber above.

Filtration Rooms Two large air intakes were built into the near-vertical eastern face of the fort in the *Tranchee de Caster*. The fresh air was forced through gas filters before being distributed to parts of the fort by a notoriously inefficient ventilation system that was in the process of being updated in May 1940.

One of the 75 mm ammunition trolleys designed to carry forty-two rounds.

The upper end of an ammunition hoist at the casemate level. The staircase to the left winds around the lift shaft.

THE UPPER LEVEL

The plateau of Saint Peter's Hill, 180 feet above the fort's entrance level, is where the offensive casemates and cupolas of Battery 1 are sited. There are also defensive features here, namely the two machine gun casemates and the four anti-aircraft machine guns.

The Maastricht and Visé Casemates On the upper surface, there were four identical concrete gun casemates, each mounting three 75 mm guns, with a range of 10,000 yards. Two were sited facing north towards Maastricht and the Albert Canal Bridges. These were known as Maastricht 1 (Ma 1) and Maastricht 2 (Ma 2) but the Germans allocated these casemates the objective numbers of 12 and 18 respectively. Facing south towards Visé were another pair of casemates Vi 1 (26) and Vi 2 (9). Each casemate was commanded by a *Sous Officer* (Sergeant

45

Maastricht 2, one of four identical casemates each mounting three 75 mm guns.

Inset: one of the 75 mm ball-mounted guns remains in position.

Major) with 4 corporals and 28 soldiers. The individual guns, fixed in steel ball mounts, had only a 70-degree arc of fire, which strictly limited their utility.

Mounted on the top of Ma 2 was Eben 3, one of the fort's three large armoured artillery observation cupolas sited on the upper surface. From here, one of the Visé Battery's artillery observation officers had an almost unrestricted view to the southeast, but could not see the Lanhay Lock.

Cupola Nord (31) and Cupola Sud (23) These two heavily armoured retracting cupolas each mounted a pair of quick-firing 75 mm guns, with a range of just 800 yards. They had a 360-degree traverse, and were raised into the firing position by a combination of electric motors and counterbalance weights. The cupolas were lowered for reloading into a protective concrete recess, leaving only the steel dome of the cupola showing above ground. As with all the fort's artillery casemates

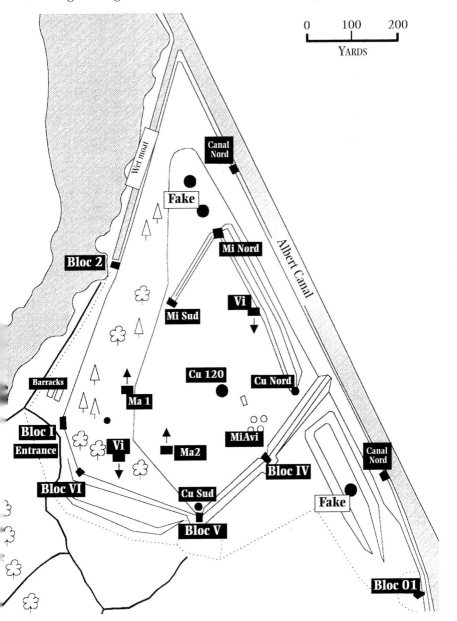

Cupola Sud elevated in its firing position.

The mechanism to raise Cupolas Sud and Nord from loading to firing position.

and cupolas, when the breaches were opened the gas defence overpressure in the chambers, maintained by the fort's ventilation system, was designed to ensure that the propellant fumes were forced out of the gun barrels rather than being vented into the cupola. Unlike the Visé and Maastricht casemates, the cupolas were constructed with three stories, the lower one having the ready store of ammunition and crew bunks. Even though Cupola Sud (23) was marked on German planning maps as being on top of Bloc V, it is thought that they had not properly identified Cupola Sud as a part of the offensive strength of the fort. Consequently, a *Fallschirmjäger* section was not allocated in the German plan to neutralise this particular position. Cupola Nord provided one of only two points of access or sally ports onto Eben Emael's upper surface.

Cupola 120 mm (24) This single heavy 300 mm thick steel cupola mounted a pair of 120 mm guns that were capable of engaging targets out to a range of almost 17,000 yards. As these were the largest guns in the fort they were given detailed fire orders by the Command Post deep in the Intermediate Level. However, target information was gathered, sifted and prioritised by I Corps's Artillery HQ before being passed to Battery 1's Command Post.

The Machine Gun Casemates – Mi Nord (19) and Mi Sud (13)
During the design process it had been anticipated that an enemy might gain a foothold on the Upper Surface by old-fashioned 'escalade' of the walls and outer defences. An airborne attack had not been envisaged. Mi Nord and Mi Sud were sited to cover approaches into the centre of the fort from the south with machine gun fire, as this was considered to be the Upper Surface's most vulnerable point. Coincidentally, these positions were well placed to cover the large open area on top of the fort that was to be used by the majority of the German gliders.

Looking out to the north, mounted on Mi Nord, was the large steel dome of the **Eben 2** artillery OP, which was manned by an observer party from the Maastricht Battery. This casemate also had the Upper Surface's second armoured sally port.

Anti-aircraft Machine guns (Mi A Avi) (29) Four open machine gun pits, grouped on the southern part of Eben Emael, were a

The massive Cupola 120 with the two barrel covers closed.

One of the two machine gun casemates covering the open Upper Surface.

Eben 2 Observation Post

part of the general air defence of the area, rather than specific protection of the fort against an air landing. However, it had been envisaged that a ground attack on the fort might be supported by aircraft or that the Germans may have sought to neutralise the fort by air bombardment while *Wehmacht* troops forced the Maastricht or Visé routes into the heart of Belgium.

Fake Cupolas (14, 16 & 32) In order to enhance the deterrent effect of the hugely expensive and arguably under-gunned fortress, three artificial cupolas of a similar size and appearance to the real 120 mm cupola were positioned on the upper surface; two in the northern part of the fortress and one south of the main defences. As we will see, the fact that the Germans attacked these positions suggests that their intelligence was not as comprehensive as has often been alleged.

Workshop (25) The large wooden and corrugated iron hanger the centre of the open area was primarily used by the fort's maintenance and repair section, but also as shelter for those working on the Upper Surface.

THE ALBERT CANAL
It was with positions on the Albert Canal stretching north from Eben Emael that the Belgians planned to hold the enemy for five days while the Allies advanced into Central Belgium and dug in on the line of the River Dyle. The canal had been deliberately designed to be a barrier to manoeuvre from the east as well as an important economic feature. It was on average 50 yards wide and 15 feet deep. The earth spoil was piled up on the western bank, so that the defenders would benefit from elevated positions from which they could dominate the open ground to the east. The Canal north of Eben Emael was a serious barrier that the Germans would have to plan to overcome, as the banks were both steep and high.

To enhance the effect of the Albert Canal as an obstacle, medium-type casemates, most with two machine gun embrasures and an embrasure for a 47 mm anti-tank gun, were built along the western bank every half mile or so. Surrounded by infantry trenches, the bunkers/strong points had overlapping arcs of fire covering the long straight stretches of canal and the barbed-wire obstacles along the banks. The canal

Lanhay Lock

Fort

Canal Nord

The Albert Canal today having been widened.

The Kanne Bridge from the east bank.

bridges were also an integral part of the defences, with some defensive casemates built into the abutments or piers. The bridges also had chambers built into the abutments and roadways, as well as holes in the superstructure to take explosive demolition charges which would be fired if a bridge was in danger of capture.

The three bridges immediately north of the fort, Kanne, Vroenhoven and Veldwezelt, were of particular importance if the Germans should seize and cross the Meuse bridges at Maastricht. The bridge at Kanne and its demolition guard of infantry was not under direct command of the Fortress

Looking north up the now widened Albert Canal cutting.

commander, Major Jottrand, but he had direct telephone communication to the firing point in **Bloc 0** which overlooked the bridge itself, doubling as an artillery OP. Major Jottrand, however, had responsibility for the destruction of the Lanhay lock gates and bridge.

Finally, there was **Bloc PL.19**, which was technically a part of the fort, being under command and connected to the Visé Battery artillery command post by telephone. This standard concrete blockhouse was sited to cover the bridges across the canal to the south of the fort in the Visé area.

SUMMARY

The Belgians had no idea that Eben Emael might be vulnerable to airborne attack, with just four anti-aircraft machine guns that in the event were inadequate. Much of the German work in developing airborne forces was secret, and the fact that the Belgians had not developed their own gliders or parachute arm led to a lack of appreciation of the developing capabilities or the possible threat to Eben Emael.

For the size and cost of the fort, there were relatively few guns, and the sixteen 75 mm and two 120 mm guns had blind spots in their coverage. In addition, the calibre of the guns at Eben Emael had been restricted so that neutral Belgium would not be seen as provocative.

The fort's ground defences lacked fully developed belts of protective barbed wire, mines, and defensive moats to protect the casemates and cupolas on the Upper Surface and the blockhouses surrounding the fort. In addition, in contrast with pre-1914 practice, the Belgians had totally dispensed with detachments of infantry at the forts and a variety of pre-prepared positions from which to fight. While the fortress was surrounded by blockhouses, the Upper Surface lacked full MG coverage. Even so, the Belgian belief that Eben Emael was impregnable lulled the garrison of artillerymen into a false sense of security, which made the shock of attack all the greater, which, in turn, did so much to fatally undermine their morale on 10/11 May 1940.

Chapter 3

GERMAN AIRBORNE AND SPECIAL FORCES

'In the present struggle for the future of our people, the German parachute troops have on every front exhibited the best soldierly virtues, great offensive spirit, and most of all an unsurpassed willingness for self-sacrifice. Wherever they fought they were the terror of the enemy.'

General der Flieger Kurt Student, 1943

German airborne forces were not a part of the core structure that was built up to support the tactical doctrine that came to be referred to as *'Blitzkrieg'*, literally translated as 'lightning war'. However, paratroopers (*Fallschirmjäger*) and other airborne troops epitomised the key *Blitzkrieg* principle of speed and risk, and also demonstrated how the nation that was defeated in 1918 was willing to embrace new ideas and technology under the leadership of Adolf Hitler.

General *der Flieger* Student, who became the most famous of the senior *Fallschirmjäger* commanders, described the events that led to the formation of the German airborne forces:

General *der Flieger* Kurt Student.

For us Germans, the concept of vertical envelopment received impetus because of two events: First were the Russian manoeuvres in 34-35, in which large numbers of paratroopers were dropped into open country. The second was in 1936 when Freiherr von Moreau's transport flights flew some of [General] *Franco's troops from Morocco to Spain with decisive effect.*

On the basis of these events, both the Army and the Luftwaffe set up parachute groups, in order to study and to test airborne operations. The results identified, in theory, three possibilities: One was that the fallschirmjäger *should be divided up into small units to jump behind the enemy's lines where they could destroy specific targets, which the* Luftwaffe *at the time were technically unable to hit. Another idea was to land directly in the enemy's rear in small units in order to give tactical support to army operations. The third possibility was that* fallschirmjäger *should carry out their own operations in larger units behind the enemy's front, without being in direct contact with the ground forces.*

Fallschirmjäger badge worn on left breast pocket.

Consequently, with the benefit of some low-level experience and with tactical doctrine in place, on 29 January 1936, orders were issued by the commander of the *Luftwaffe* to form the 7th Flying (*Flieger*) Division under its first commander, General *der Flieger* Kurt Student. His plan for the division was to raise a force of three regiments (equivalent to

Fallschirmjäger taking part in Hitler's birthday parade. Inset: Luftwaffe eagle worn above right breast pocket.

British brigades), one of which would be fully parachute trained, with the other two regiments being 'air-landing'. Student explained that:

> *The* Wehrmacht *provided the 16th Infantry Regiment and handed it over to me, as far as tactics and training were concerned. However, a second regiment could not be provided, and we were helped by an unusual idea: Göring, who knew the SA well, took the leaders and*

Fallschirmjäger during pre-war training.

> *the best men from that organisation and moved them without more ado into the* Luftwaffe.

In this way General Student also successfully acquired the necessary men to set up a third regiment within a matter of months. With the infantry strength for a whole division now available, intensive training on the exercise grounds began.

The Division's order of battle (ORBAT), to the envy of airborne forces since that time, was completed by the permanent assignment of both transport and offensive air-support units. Firstly, there were two transport squadrons of Ju 52 aircraft, one squadron of fighter aircraft, one of bombers, and a recce squadron. In addition, to complete the ground ORBAT, there was a *Luftwaffe* signal battalion, a strong medical group and other

supporting arms necessary for operating in isolation. The division was raised on the expectation that it would fight with light scales, depending heavily on air support. However, as aircraft and equipment were developed, the *Flieger* Division's support elements grew in both number and combat power.

German airborne forces expanded until by the spring of 1940 they represented a powerful force. Winston Churchill, in power for only a matter of weeks, ordered the first British experiments with parachuting in June 1940, following the German example of how to effectively use this new arm.

Gliders

The Germans were severely restricted by the Versailles Treaty in the field of military aircraft, including troop transports. Consequently, as *Reichsmarschall* Herman Göring explained in the early 1920s, there was to be an emphasis on the glider as the foundation of the future German *Luftwaffe*; and therefore, by the mid-1930s, sport gliding and

Herman Göring, air ace of the Great War. As a member of the Nazi party he became the founder of the *Luftwaffe*.

glider technology was well established across Germany.

After Hitler had witnessed some spectacular displays of formation flying and pin-point landing, later he met Professor Georgie from the Research Institute of Gliding at the Dramstadt technical college in 1936, and the concept of a military utility for gliders came into his mind. When Professor Georgie returned to his laboratory and workshop, he tasked his flight construction manager Hans Jacobs to look at the problem.

This question naturally came as a great surprise to me. Up until then we had only developed various types for sport gliding, so it was rather difficult to answer the question. However, my thoughts followed this line: a glider towed up to 6,000 – 9,000 feet can, with an angle of descent of 1 in 18, fly silently for tens of kilometres into enemy territory, all of this in the morning twilight so that the plane cannot be seen. So the idea of deploying the military glider had been born.

At the beginning of 1937, after some theoretical designs had been produced, orders were issued by the Reich's Aviation Ministry to build a mock up of an aircraft, which could carry the pilot and up to nine armed and equipped soldiers. This dummy was viewed by representatives of the Ministry, and an order followed immediately for the construction of three prototype aircraft.

A DFS 230 glider under tow with a Junkers 87 Stuka dive bomber as escort. Note the MG 34 light machine gun fitted on top of later versions.

The Junkers 52 (Ju 52) used as a tug aircraft.

A military troop-carrying glider was by no means unanimously considered useful (and the *Fallschirmjäger* regarded gliders as unwelcome competition for resources), but the more visionary commanders prevailed. They saw that its foremost advantage was its ability to land troops together rather than spread out over several hundred yards. Another feature that appealed to the *Luftwaffe* was a glider's ability to make a silent approach.

Work on a military glider began promptly in March 1937 at Dramstadt, based on converting existing designs, and setting up an experimental flight, along with a training command, to gain experience in the *Luftwaffe's* newest aircraft – the 'Attack Glide'.

Colonel Mrazek described the continuing debate over the usefulness of the glider from a military point of view:

A second demonstration was held, this time before the Army General Staff. Ten Junkers [Ju] 52s transporting paratroopers, and ten gliders carrying glidermen towed behind ten more Ju 52s, flew to the airfield at Stendal. There the gliders were cast off, and the paratroopers dropped. The gliders dived steeply and came to rest in close formation, discharging glidermen in units ready to fight. On the other hand, the parachutists, who had the ill luck to encounter a stiff breeze, from which the gliders had actually benefited, landed widely dispersed, in some cases a considerable distance from their ammunition, which had been dropped by parachute. Though this experiment could not, of course, obscure the importance of paratroopers in a future war, it at least proved conclusively that the troop-carrying glider could become a weapon of great value.

Full production of the DFS 230 Attack Glider began at the Gotha aircraft plant, while the *Luftwaffe* began to train its first 60 military glider pilots for operations on the prototypes and the first production gliders.

THE DFS 230 GLIDER

The basis of the DFS 230's design was a meteorological aircraft that was essentially a small engineless transport, which during the redesign process lost its sleek curves and long

elegant wings. The result was a short airframe and stubby wings, designed to bear weight and provide sufficient lift for the glider to descend steadily from its release point to its objective. What proved to be impossible was for the loaded aircraft to ride thermals and to remain soaring for protracted periods, as a sport glider would.

A summary of the technical details follows:

A glider and a Ju 52 combination.

Fallschirmjäger **demonstrate a quick exit from a DFS 230 glider during training.**

Fuselage: Covered with a painted canvas fabric, the DFS 230's fuselage was made up of a framework of steel tubing capable of accommodating a pilot and eight or nine men and equipment, giving a total payload of 2,800 pounds. The aircraft eventually had a position for a light machine gun in a slit in the fuselage on the starboard side.

Undercarriage: The fuselage had wheels for taking off which were normally jettisoned after take-off. These could be retained should the glider be returning to a nicely manicured airfield, but for tactical landings, the DFS 230 would land on a skid fixed below its fuselage.

Wings: With a span of 72 feet and a surface area of 444 square feet, the DFS 230's wings were constructed in traditional glider manner from plywood, which was covered with the same canvas fabric as the fuselage. The DFS 230 had a high wing design braced from the fuselage.

Braking mechanism: For tactical landing the glider relied on friction to bring it to a halt. Eben Emael's assault force, training over winter, tried to enhance the friction by wrapping barbed wire around the skid, but eventually resorted to a saw-toothed braking device. Braking rockets and drogue parachutes were fitted to later models of the DFS 230.

Weight: Empty: 2,800 pounds. Laden weight: 4,600 pounds.

Flying speed: The optimum speed for towing was 120 miles an hour, with a similar speed for the glide down to the landing zone.

GERMAN 'SPECIAL FORCES'

A key aspect of the German *Blitzkrieg* was the rapid advance of the panzer divisions. Mindful of how the Allies had halted the German 1918 offensives, which tended to run out of steam against relatively small groups of men holding key points deep in what had been the enemy's rear area, the *Wehrmacht* developed the world's first 'Special Forces' unit.

It was apparent early in the planning process that operations to capture or at least deny the destruction of key points (such as bridges in enemy territory) would be necessary during the opening phase of the offensive in the west. It was essential to maintain the tempo of operations by allowing the panzer divisions to strike deep into France, Belgium and Holland in order to allow the armoured torrent to expand and produce the desired Allied collapse. The problem was that the Germans' routes across the flat country of Belgium and Holland were barred by numerous waterways, ranging from canals such as the Albert to major rivers such as the Meuse/Maas and the Schelde. In addition, there were key points such as Eben Emael, and further south, important junctions to be seized in the difficult terrain of the Ardennes.

The response to this tactical problem was to expand the number of commando-type troops that had played a small part in the 1939 invasion of Poland, by raising a Special Forces battalion under the cover of being a training and construction unit. It was designated the Brau-Lehr Battalion z.b.V. ('Special Purposes') 800. However, mainly as a cover, the Battalion soon took the name 'Brandenburgers' after the town outside Berlin where they were stationed.

From the earliest days, the Brandenburgers' selection and training emphasised qualities and features that are easily recognisable in today's Special Forces. A ready supply of men suitable to work behind enemy lines was available from amongst the *Volksdeutsche* of the provinces lost to Belgium and France after the Great War. These soldiers could easily pass themselves off as French or Flemish, but language skills were not enough. Brandenburg soldiers also had to display an ability to think independently and be both mentally and physically resilient: without these qualities, entry into the Battalion would be denied.

The soldiers were trained in a wide range of skills, from traditional activities such as skill at arms and night operations, to parachuting and small boat handling, to survival training where they would have to live off the land. The Brandenburgers quickly developed into an elite unit whose skills were employed in the coming attack.

OBJECTIVES AND METHODS

As the plan for the attack in the west matured, the Brandenburgers' training for what was to become known as Operation *Niwi* was focused on their specific objectives. However, other groups were raised for similar specific purposes, from divisions such as *Gross Deutschland* and from the ordinary infantry of 34th Division. They developed and practised insertion methods; not just parachuting into the operational area, but being flown in, in small numbers, by Fiesler Storchs aircraft; or dressed in enemy uniforms and infiltrating into the objective, typically, as we will see, by bicycle. In some cases, infiltration would begin the day before

Fiesler Storch used for insertion activities during the invasion of France.

ENGAGEZ-VOUS
RENGAGEZ-VOUS

DANS LES
TROUPES
MÉTROPOLITAINES

The French had the Maginot Line and the Belgians their series of forts to protect their countries from invasion by the Germans.

Brandenburg men in training prior to the attack in the West in 1940.

A rare photograph of German Special Forces disguised as Dutch policemen having just taken part in the successful capture of a bridge in May 1940.

the main attack, and in others, overnight. Finally, a hundred Storchs aircraft would make two sorties into the enemy's rear, carrying two Brandenburgers on each trip.

In preparation for action in the area of the objective, the Brandenburgers were trained to attack and seize their specific objectives, and once these were captured, to conduct their own demolitions or to neutralise those of the enemy. Another aim of Operation *Niwi* was to spread confusion in the enemy rear area. Of course, the very presence of the Brandenburgers would contribute to this, but they would also cut telephone lines, ambush staff cars, etc. In some cases, activities such as felling trees to block routes proved to be as much of a nuisance to their own side as to the enemy. Skilful use of long-range (high-frequency) radio communications to report success, failure or indeed enemy movements to the advancing formations was essential. Finally, the Battalion was trained in the conventional capability to hold their key points against counter-attack until relieved by the German armoured spearheads.

Operation *Niwi* and other special-forces operations were, in the event, not universally successful, but they were successful enough to attract attention from other nations, who began setting up their own special forces or commando units to carry out similar roles.

Chapter 4

GERMAN PLANS FOR INVASION OF THE WEST

After their defeat in 1918, the Germans analysed their reasons for failure, and looked at their geopolitical situation. Still sandwiched between victorious France and philosophically hostile Soviet Russia, the problem of avoiding war on two fronts remained. Also to be avoided was an attritional war, which, against the superior manpower resources and economic power of her combined potential enemies, Germany was bound to lose.

The solution was to develop political alliances and armed forces capable of delivering prompt victory. The technology and tactics that were beginning to emerge in 1917 and 1918 provided the basis for development. While Britain rested on its laurels, cut back defence spending, tended to resume its 'obsession with the horse', and did its best to ignore military theorists such as Fuller and Liddle Hart, the French drew the conclusion from the Great War that modern weapons had made a war of manoeuvre impossible to sustain on a large scale. In contrast to France, who spent 2.9 billion francs between the years 1929 – 1932 on building the Maginot Line defences, Germany set about forging a new style of warfare.

Part of the Maginot Line defence system at Lembach in the Vosges. French troops take a breath of fresh air.

Hitler saw the need for a different kind of warfare.

Blitzkrieg

Hitler promptly broke free from the Versailles restrictions when he came to power in 1933. Re-armament produced a new range of modern and capable weapon systems. Using armour and motorised troops in a way that exploited their mobility, fire power and speed of manoeuvre on the battlefield was seen as a way of avoiding attritional war and gaining swift knockout victories that would preclude Germany from becoming bogged down in fighting on two fronts. The Germans developed a tactical doctrine for the *Wehrmacht's* armoured and motorised spearhead (the majority of the Army remained on foot or horse-drawn) which combined panzers, motorised infantry and supporting arms with close air-support aircraft and with special forces. One of the chief armoured theorists, General Guderian, with a signals background in the Great War, stressed the importance of effective radio communications in order to exploit even the most fleeting of battlefield opportunities. To make this new tactical doctrine work, commanders at all levels were required to act independently, with initiative, within a broad framework of orders and objectives. After the successful campaign in Poland during September 1939, the new Germans' tactical doctrine was dubbed by a journalist *'Blitzkrieg' or 'Lightning War'*.

Warsaw fell and Poland surrendered after a gratifyingly short campaign on 27 September. Hitler quickly announced his intention to attack the British and French as soon as possible, and on 9 October 1939 he issued Führer Directive Number 6, which gave the operational framework for the plans that were to be prepared for a campaign in the west. The document

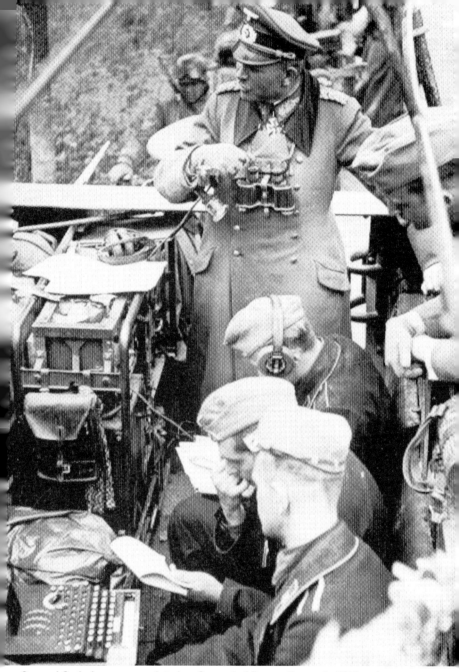

General Guderian was appointed as General of Panzer Troops in 1938 and authored the book *Achtung! Panzer*. With the innovative new form of warfare he stressed the importance of effective radio communications. Here he is seen in his corps command truck in May 1940.

outlined Hitler's aim to defeat,

> *as much as possible of the French Army and the allies fighting on their side ... gaining as much territory as possible in the Netherlands, Belgium and northern France, to serve as a base for the prosecution of an air and sea war against England and provide a wide protective area for the economically vital Ruhr.*

The German High Command's initial response was largely based on the Schlieffen Plan that their forbears had attempted to execute in 1914. In the 1939 version, known as *der Fall Gelb* (Case Yellow), the panzer divisions of Army Group B were to launch the main attack (*Schwerpunkt*) across the northern plains of Belgium, while the infantry of Army Group A would make a diversionary attack in the Ardennes. Further to the south, along the Franco-German border, Army Group C would fix the French army in place in and around the Maginot Line. The presence of the fortress of Eben Emael and the Albert Canal defence line facing the *Schwerpunkt* was, as we will see, a significant factor in this plan.

Within this general framework, there were several changes in plan, and proposals to redirect the *Schwerpunkt* within the frontage to be attacked by Army Group B. There is evidence, however, that towards the end of October 1939 Hitler proposed that a subsidiary attack by a panzer and a panzer-grenadier division should be launched through the Ardennes to the Meuse at Sedan. This was probably the result of criticism that an attack into Belgium and northern France would not deliver the desired knock-out blow, and that to do so, the *Schwerpunkt* should be further south. Despite his generals' criticism of *Fall Gelb*, on 5 November 1939, Hitler issued orders that *Angriffstag* (attack-day) would be on 12 November. The plan was more or less the original: the main armoured thrust advancing through northern Belgium being delivered by Army Group B. Two days later, however, the operation was cancelled for the first of numerous times over the winter of 1939-40. Further Führer orders followed, refining the plan and incorporating options such as the capture of Holland.

Commander Army Group B *Feldmarschall* von Rundstedt and his Chief of Staff, General von Manstein, repeatedly pressed the case that *Fall Gelb's Schwerpunkt* should be further south, but the head of the Army High Command (OKH), *Feldmarschall* von Brauchitsch, was not convinced, and *Fall Gelb* remained

Operations in Belgium and Holland - May 1940.

substantially unaltered. OKH did, however, concede that the attack's main effort would be adjusted in accordance with the enemy's disposition of his forces and how the battle developed.

Thus the situation remained until February, when a transport plane became lost in bad weather and was forced down with a copy of an operation order that revealed to the Allies that the intended German *Schwerpunkt* lay through northern Belgium. This event forced Hitler to reconsider the von Manstein plan, which was duly adopted. Fortunately for the Germans, the Allies thought that the loss of the plan was a ruse designed to mislead them, and remained convinced that the main effort would lie with Army Group A in the north.

The new and final version of the plan was also called *Fall Gelb*. It reversed the roles of Army Groups B and A. Army Group B, spearheaded by the majority of the panzer divisions, would attack through the Ardennes, cross the Meuse and envelope the British and French in northern France. Meanwhile, Army Group A was now tasked to conduct a feint operation in Belgium and to capture Holland, which was designed to attract the enemy deeper into the envelopment. This meant that Eben Emael was no longer sited on the German *Schwerpunkt*. However, for the plan to succeed, the Allies had to believe, during the vital early days of the offensive, that the main threat was the German advance into Belgium and consequently, Eben Emael would still have to be taken, to allow the threat to develop convincingly.

Plans for Eben Emael
During the initial OKH intelligence briefings and estimate process, neutralising the Belgian fortress of Eben Emael, so that the panzer divisions could roll across the Maastricht and Albert Canal bridges and on into central Belgium, was of pivotal importance. Hitler was not satisfied that the Sixth Army's spearheads could guarantee to capture both fort and bridges without a serious delay and a loss of operational tempo. So on 21 October 1939 the instruction that Eben Emael should be taken by *fallschirmjäger* was formally added to the draft plan. Hitler dwelt on this requirement for several days before, at midday on 27 October, ordering *Reichsmarschall* Göring to send General *der Flieger* Student to see him in the Reichs Chancellery 'alone and without delay'.

Hitler at the time of Operation *Gelb*, conferring with his Army Commander-in-Chief von Brauchitsch (left) and his chief of the OKW, Keitel (right). This was the front page of *Die Wehrmacht* magazine in 1940.

As a Great War pilot, Student himself flew the short distance to Berlin in his personal Fiesler Storchs aircraft. Even the *Reichsmarschall* was made to wait outside in the ante-chamber while Student went into Hitler's office on his own. General Student recalled:

The Führer had a map spread on his desk. He began "The war in the west," paused, and then asked, "You have trained with gliders and have some in your division?" I agreed, and he continued "Then I have a task for you and I want to know if you can carry it out. The Belgians have a fort at Eben Emael: do you know it?" I replied that it was the most serious of all the border defences we faced.

Hitler then gave me a detailed description of the fort and how it would affect the plan. "The top of the fort is a large grass open area, with

General *der Flieger* Kurt Student.

surface positions. I have information that there are heavy artillery gun cupolas and casemates, with some machine guns. But I have no extensive details."

He then told me that he had read my reports on the DFS 230 attack glider and that he knew I was a glider pilot and that I had personally flown the glider. The Führer *then came to the point. "I have a thought. I believe that your attack gliders could land on top of the Fort and your* fallschirmjäger *could attack these positions. Is that possible?" I replied that "I need time to think about it."*

It was a daunting proposition but it had an elegant simplicity. Hitler dismissed Student but required him to come back with a prompt answer, as the original proposed date of the attack on the west was only two weeks away. Student was back in the Chancellery the next day.

Pleasantries were brief and I told Hitler what he wanted to hear. I said "Yes, my Führer. It is possible under specific circumstances. The landings must be made in daylight - at least dawn - not before." Hitler promptly replied "Good! It will be done your way," and I asked, "May I have your order, my Führer?"

However, Student's briefing was not over, and the Führer directed him to a chair. Hitler then seemingly went into a reverie about the Great War, and talked about how, as a soldier, he remembered hearing how French and Belgian fortifications had held out against repeated attacks. It was not until the Germans deployed siege guns to destroy the fort that the garrison surrendered. Hitler believed that it was 'not German heroism that had prevailed but it was super heavy shells that finally broke enemy resistance.' This reverie was, however, only the preamble to Hitler's revelation of another of the Reich's secrets.

The Hollow Charge

Hitler came to the point and described to Student the *Hohlladung* (hollow charge), which had been developed by German explosive engineers. The charge was capable of blasting its way through the thick stone, concrete and steel used in a modern fortress.

Lieutenant Colonel Thomas Mouat, a British Army ammunition technical officer, explains how the hollow charge worked:

The mechanism of the charge was designed to use the "Munroe Effect", first discovered in America in 1888. Munroe noticed that the manufacturer's details, engraved into the surface of a slab of explosive, produced engraved reflections in the surface of the metal he was trying to blow up. He experimented with cutting cavities into explosive charges, and was amazed to discover these cavities produced cavities of their own in their target (the Munroe Effect).

Modern charges make use of a liner inside the cavity of a dense and malleable material which is formed by the force of the explosion into a jet of material that blasts its way through the target. ... The effect of this cavity liner was not fully understood in 1939, and it was not appreciated what a difference the angle

30kg Hollow charge

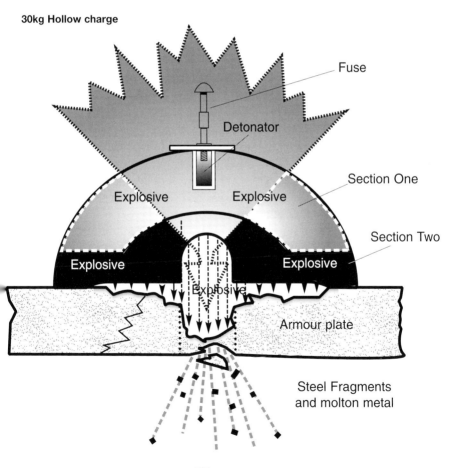

The effect of a 50 kilo hollow charge on one of Eben Emael's steel cupolas.

*and shape of the cavity, and choice of material of the liner, would
make to the penetrating power.*

*The "Munroe Effect" charges were far more effective than
conventional explosives in attacking concrete and armour plate
when the thickness of the armour was less than the cavity size in
the charge.*

The larger 50 kilogram charges, in experimental conditions, had
penetrated 25 centimetres of armour plate or 35 centimetres of
concrete, and the 12.5kg charge, 12 to 15 centimetres of steel.
However, the problem was that they were both bulky and
heavy, which meant that they had to be placed and the 10-
second fuse initiated by hand. The 50kg charge came in two
sections, which had to be assembled on site. Hitler told Student,
'If they can be delivered to the enemy positions, then nothing,
nothing can withstand it.' This revelation provided General
Student with the answer to how a few glider loads of lightly
armed *fallschirmjäger*, equipped with conventional explosives,
could neutralise Eben Emael's casemates. Hitler believed that
this combination of the glider and the hollow charge provided
him with the solution to the seemingly all-powerful fortress.

Having told Student 'I order you to take Fort Eben Emael and
the three Albert Canal bridges' and that these verbal orders

were to be acted on, Hitler reminded Student that 'all aspects of the operation must be kept absolutely secret!' It is worth stressing from the outset that the seizure of the bridges was to be the main effort, as without the bridges the prompt capture of Eben Emael would have been worthless. In addition to the fort and the canal bridges, Student was given outline details of the task for his 7th *Flieger* Division and the 22nd Infantry Division. They were to take the key points in the Netherlands and the Belgian national redoubt by descent and hold them until the *Wehrmacht* arrived.

Sturmabteilung Koch

With only a short time to organise and prepare his assault force, General Student lost no time in allocating troops to the tasks that he had been given. His selection for the overall commander was *Hauptmann* Koch, a company commander in 1st *Fallschirmjäger* Regiment. This young officer was an inspirational leader and an extremely inventive commander. The choice of the officer to attack Eben Emael itself was easier, as *Leutnant* Witzig, commander of the 7th *Flieger* Division's engineer or 'pioneer' *Kompanie*, already led the *fallschirmjäger, who* would be placing the hollow charges. The commander of the glider element of the force was to be *Leutnant* Kees.

Hauptmann **Koch.**

On 30 October 1939, Koch, Witzig and Kees were summoned to Berlin for orders at Headquarters 7th *Flieger* Division. *Leutnant* Witzig recalled:

> *The orders that General Student gave us were that a* Sturmabteilung *is to be set up under the command of* Hauptmann *Koch, who had up to then been commander of the* 1st Kompanie *of* Fallschirmjäger Regiment 1. My Fallschirmjäger *pioneer* Kompanie, *the only one we had at the time, was to join the* Abteilung *and be answerable to* Hauptmann *Koch.*

Oberleutnant **Witzig.**

> *Student told us that there were three bridges over the Albert Canal to be taken and the Eben Emael fort to be silenced.*

Leutnant Kees was happy that while 7th *Flieger* Division's glider pilots could be relied on at the canal-bridge objectives, he realised that he would have to have the very best pilots

77

Fallschirmjäger training with rubber boats.

available to land on the restricted upper surface of the Fort. As a priority operation, he knew that he could chose whoever he wanted for the operation. Heiner Lange was one of those who received a new assignment:

It was on 8 November 1939, when I was then temporarily training pilots in Guben, that I got my marching orders to Hildersheim. I arrived in the grey light of dawn and reported to the airfield, where I was sent to some quarters. Here I met three old glider-training friends, Kraft, Brautigam and Ziller; they were surprised to see me and told me a little about the operation, which was very surprising. Afterwards, I went out onto the airfield to look at the DFS 230 gliders on the ground, which was the first time I saw the ten-seater aircraft. I knew nothing of their existence before this!

Not all the glider pilots were as willing as Lange, but they had a degree of 'choice' as the demands and manpower controls of total war were yet to manifest themselves. Some of the best sport-glider pilots had to be 'persuaded' that in becoming a temporary member of the *Luftwaffe* they would be carrying out a significant service to their country. Having volunteered, not only did they discover that they were to fly in one of military history's most audacious raids but they were also expected to fight as infantrymen.

Sturmabteilung Koch assembled in a barracks at Hildersheim under a variety of innocent-sounding names, where for the sake of security they were to be kept in strict isolation until the operation was mounted. There was no leave, and according to *Leutnant* Witzig 'nor were we allowed out or to mix with men from other units'. He continued:

Of course we no longer wore our paratroopers uniform on training, and we had no signs of rank. There were many of these types of measure over the months, and Hauptmann *Koch had to keep thinking of something else to preserve security.*

Fallschirmjäger **practise exiting the DFS 230 glider and going straight into the attack.**

> *Undoubtedly his measures were a success, as our enemy knew nothing and suspected nothing of our orders, of our capabilities or of our operations. Consequently, we succeeded in gaining technical and tactical surprise.*

From the outset, the force, numbering 400 mainly *fallschirmjäger*, was divided into task groups reflecting their objectives. *Sturmgruppe Stahl* (Storm Group Steel) was to seize the most northerly of the three road bridges west of Maastricht, at Veldwezelt; *Sturmgruppe Beton* (Concrete) was assigned that at Vroenhoven; and the bridge nearest the fort at Kanne went to *Sturmgruppe Eisen* (Iron). *Sturmgruppe Granit* (Granite), at eighty men the largest of the storm groups, was commanded by a pioneer officer *Leutnant* Witzig. A group of dummy parachutists was to be dropped beyond Eben Emael to act as a distraction and to help paralyse Belgian command. *Sturmabteilung* Koch's task was to hold the bridges and neutralise Eben Emael's artillery casemates and cupolas until relieved by a force that would complete the capture of the fort.

Sturmgruppe Granit's Plan and Training
While *Hauptmann* Koch and the remainder of the *Sturmabteilung* were landing at the bridges to the north, *Leutnant* Witzig's *Sturmgruppe* would be landing on the open upper surface of the

Fort in eleven DFS 230 Assault Gliders. In order to carry out his mission of neutralising Eben Emael's offensive firepower, nine of Witzig's eleven sections were to attack the main artillery casemates and cupolas, including the two northern cupolas (objectives 14 and 16) that turned out to be fakes. He recorded that:

> *Our study of aerial photographs and a relief model had convinced us that our initial assault had to be restricted to the central casemates. First, we were to destroy all infantry weapons and anti-aircraft guns firing in the open, and after that the artillery, particularly where directed to the north.*

Fallschirmjäger of **Sturmabteilung Koch** on their assault course at Hildesheim.

> *Speed was essential, since anything not accomplished in the first 60 minutes would be made practically impossible later by the increasing strength of enemy defence.*

His remaining two gliders carried the two radiomen and the two reserves sections, trained to take the place of any of the other sections who for whatever reason failed to reach the fort. Having landed, the assault sections' immediate task was to attack their objectives with the hollow charges and destroy the guns. As an insurance policy, the *Sturmgruppe* also had smaller conventional demolition charges and flamethrowers.

The *fallschirmjäger* were told that they could expect to see the spearheads of 4th Panzer Division, having travelled 20 miles across Holland, including the River Meuse at Maastricht, crossing into the Albert Canal bridgeheads within six hours of their initial landing. The plan was that 51st Pioneer Battalion and 151 Infantry Regiment would complete the capture of the fortress by subduing the defensive blockhouses surrounding Eben Emael.

However, the plan was not to be put into operation in 1939, as a senior *Luftwaffe* officer reported, because the immediate

Lanaye Locks

Bloc 0I

Albert Canal

Dry moat

Bloc V

14 and 16

Wet moat

Bloc I

N

deadline slipped, in a series of delays that kept *Sturmabteilung* Koch poised on a knife-edge of readiness throughout much of the winter.

Originally the attack was supposed to have taken place in November 1939, but some of the best-known commanders protested against this, and in any case the bad winter weather was a good reason for not deploying the *Luftwaffe* in support of the ground forces in such unfavourable conditions. Therefore, Hitler gave in and postponed the attack until spring. That of course was a great good fortune for the *fallschirmjäger*, because everything necessary for the operation could be practised and learned during intensive training sessions in the winter months.

Given the complexity of the attack on Eben Emael, it was unlikely to have been successfully carried out at short notice, with little training and scant coordination. As a result of the delay, the *fallschirmjäger* trained to fight together and repeatedly practised taking over the task of another part of their group. *Leutnant* Witzig, who was to command *Sturmgruppe Granit*, described the information on which the training was based:

> *We theoretically knew the procedures to attack fortresses, but at first there were only a few documents, photos and aerial photos of the fort; but later we had more, including pairs of photographs for stereoscopic evaluation. Then we began making a sand model, but this was replaced by a proper detailed model made by one of our glider pilots, Ziller I think, who happened to be a specialist in the art. He was quite a famous pilot as well!*

Each position on the upper surface of Eben Emael, identified from the air photographs and other intelligence including Belgian deserters, be it an artillery casemate or a cupola, was allocated a number (shown in brackets after the Belgian name throughout this book). *Sturmgruppe Granit's* eleven gliders, each carrying a pilot plus seven or eight men, were allocated an objective. Pioneer Sergeant Major, *Oberfeldwebel* Wenzel recounted that:

> *Again and again we went over the plans on our models made up from the recce photos and we also laid down the dimensions of the fort on our training area and marked out our objectives according to our aerial photos.*

Oberfeldwebel Wenzel recalled the *Sturmgruppe's* early training, 'We sat down in the landing position, and on a whistle blast that was supposed to signify the landing, we jumped up and raced

Panzer troops training at Sennelager in March 1940. The NCO with the white band on his helmet is an umpire.

Practising attacking casemates using a flamethrower.

to our objectives and attacked them.'

However, the Hildesheim training area had its limitations, lacking realism and real concrete casemates and cupolas to attack. *Hauptmann* Koch sought out suitable areas to practise on. Probably the best fortifications in Europe, those on the Czechoslovakian Sudetenland border, had fallen without a shot being fired and were consequently available for training *Sturmgruppe* Witzig. A feature similar to Saint Peter's Hill was also located near Stolberg in Germany and turned into a temporary training area.

In great secrecy, Witzig's men, including the pilots, were trained in the use of the hollow charges at the *Wehrmacht* Pioneer School at Karlshorst, before practical exercises in the use of the two sizes of charge against the Polish border fortifications, which had been overrun just a few months earlier. In these training areas, according to *Leutnant* Witzig:

It was then possible to divide the whole Kompanie, *and position them on the surface of the mock fort where they were to land. From these points, within sight of the objectives, they practised the quick short attacking run-up to their targets.*

A-Tag was constantly delayed, but our time was fully occupied in practising new techniques, such as pin-point landings with explosive on the airstrip and in open country, or rapid disembarkation when fully armed. In addition to flamethrowers and the collapsible assault ladders that we built ourselves, the special equipment for the operation consisted chiefly of 2^1/$_2$ tons of explosive, predominantly hollow charges.

After a winter of training and the return of more predictable campaign weather, on 5 March *Hauptmann* Koch and *Leutnant* Witzig presented Hitler with their battle plans in Berlin. The Führer pronounced himself satisfied, and after six months of training and isolation, *Sturmabteilung* Koch was ready to go. However, there were another two months of waiting, including a period starting on 9 April 1940 while German troops invaded Denmark and Norway, before the final code words to initiate *Fall Gelb* in the west were finally issued.

Chapter 5

THE FLY IN

Soldiers of the Western Front. The hour has now arrived for you. The battle beginning today will decide the fate of the German nation for the next thousand years.
ADOLF HITLER'S ORDER OF THE DAY, 10 MAY 1940

With the prospect of improving weather came orders for *Sturmabteilung* Koch to move from their isolation at Hildersheim to what was to become the western theatre of operations. Their final home was the anti-aircraft barracks at Hilden, on the outskirts of Dusseldorf, while the gliders, which had been dismantled in January 1940 and transported along specially closed autobahns, waited at airfields near Köln. Here, in remote fenced and guarded hangars, the DFS 230's were put through final preparations for the operation.

As a cover, because even the station commanders did not know what was going on in the hangars, rumours of large-scale smoke-generation experiments were deliberately circulated. At one airfield, however, a pair of curious *Luftwaffe* guards wandered too close to the hangar, and were promptly

Hitler and his staff in 1940.

incarcerated by *Hauptmann* Koch until after the operation. In addition, two of Koch's own men were in trouble for fraternising with anti-aircraft gunners at Hilden; they were 'sentenced to be executed' as an example, but were only confined until the operation was under way. With the rush to be ready, after the move west behind them, Koch's men had now only to wait for Hitler's political moment to be right.

OKH finally issued the codeword *'Gelb'* (yellow) at 1200 hours on 9 May 1940, ending weeks of tension. *Sturmabteilung* Koch, in the confines of their barracks at Hilden, received the notification at 1420 hours. After the war, a senior *Luftwaffe* officer described the reaction of the *fallschirmjäger*:

The final operational command on 9 May came as a relief to the troops. The troops had no moral or political objections to the attack in the west, because the German propaganda had convinced them that this attack was just and right. The orders had all been prepared and sent to the troops, so that after the codeword there was not much left to organise.'

For *Gefreiter* Alefs, however, 9 May was the beginning of the most memorable period of his life:

Everything had gone as usual that fateful day... A serene, peaceful Germany prevailed... Then it came, not as we had expected. Most of us happened to be close by, and looked at one another knowingly. I glanced at Schultz and Hoepfner. We had been confined for months and had been transformed into killers. Everything we had done was in preparation for this hour! Feldwebel Heinemann didn't line us up like tin soldiers ... He walked from one to the other like a father. He said, "It is tomorrow!"

I remember my knees trembled. Why they did, I don't know. There was no danger, no shouting – only a great quiet.

For security reasons the *fallschirmjäger* **did not wear their distinctive uniforms, helmet and insignia until the eve of their departure.**

Sturmabteilung Koch reached its two airfields, Köln-Ostheim and Köln-Butzweilerhof by 1830 hours. The men were ordered to write their last letters home, replace their *fallschirmjäger* insignia, and have a last look over their personal equipment.

In the hangar at Ostheim, *Sturmgruppe* Granit received the final confirmation that the operation was on and that there would be no recall. Codeword 'Danzig' was issued by OKH at 2100 hours. The *Luftwaffe* ground crews appeared shortly afterwards, followed by the arrival of the Ju 52s that lined up on the runway. For the *fallschirmjäger* and the pilots, waiting in the hangar, it was time to prepare the gliders. Heiner Lange commented:

> *There we were appointed to our operational machines, which were standing ready for take-off. Every pilot supervised the loading of equipment belonging to his group of* Fallschirmjäger, *weapons, ammunition and explosives. Under the watchful eye of the pilot, we had to ensure that the machine remained airworthy, especially because of the weight. After this loading, we were called together and given our final operational orders, confirming our exact objectives, which we had already worked out from the models at Hildesheim. It was confirmed that our objective was indeed in Belgium.*

Leutnant Witzig recalled that,

> *There weren't many orders to give; the plans were well known and understood. The only detail remaining was the timings; when we would have supper and when we would be woken and have breakfast. In the event, most were already awake. Finally, I told them the times to parade by the aircraft, which would be in the dark on the runway, and the last boarding time.*
>
> *The mood of our soldiers: they weren't noisy; every man was serious and composed, every one was aware of what he was facing. But every man was equally convinced that he would do his utmost to carry out his orders.*

Confined to the tension-charged hangar, appetite deserted

many of the men, and, as Witzig implied, most were only able to doze briefly before reveille. Others, as soldiers have done for many years and indeed still do, played cards to distract themselves as the hours before the operation dragged by.

The *fallschirmjäger* were called from their beds at 0300 hours. *Leutnant* Witzig wrote:

> *0435 hours was our departure time: this was precisely calculated to allow our four Sturmgruppe to land simultaneously, at 0525 hours, at the bridges and at Eben Emael -- five minutes before the army crossed the frontier. We proceeded to our gliders, climbed aboard and the transport Ju 52s started up.*

Gefreiter Alefs, who had walked out to the glider and tow aircraft with a 7 Section sign illuminated by a hurricane lamp, recounted:

> *The glider began rocking as the pilots of the Ju 52 revved the engines, whose roar was muffled by the now tightly closed glider. We didn't take off at once. There were many other planes and gliders to take off ahead of us, that I could hear roaring as they went down the runway.*
>
> *Suddenly, a jerk on our tow-rope forced me backwards and there was a pitching and yawing motion as the tow rope tightened and swung the glider in behind the plane ahead. Simultaneously, we all started the chant of the parachutists, "The sun shines red, be ready...'*

Leaving a Ju 52 on the day of the invasion of the Low Countries.

> *As we picked up speed, the wobbling of the wheels, the slapping of the propeller wash against the fuselage, drowned us out. ... We were on our way!*

By 0335 hours the last glider was off the ground, and gaining height by circling to the south; then the sixty combinations of glider and Ju 52 turned westwards, following a marked route. *Oberfeldwebel* Wenzel reported that:

> *Everything went normally until we reached a height where a Ju 52 plane from* Sturmgruppe *Stahl flew close over us; we ducked our heads and had a few doubts about the success of the operation.*
>
> *We flew along the illuminated path to the border, where every 20 kilometres a searchlight had been set up.*

The blue beams of the searchlights were set up to bring the two streams of aircraft together, *Sturmgruppe* Stahl from Butzweilerhof, northwest of Köln, and the remainder of the *Sturmabteilung* from Ostheim. Despite Wenzel's near miss, for most the 50-minute flight to Eben Emael was routine. However, the already slim force of eighty-five *fallschirmjäger* pioneers and glider pilots was reduced by two sections when a pair of aircraft were forced down.

The first glider to lose its tow, piloted by *Gefreiter* Pilz, was one of the reserve-section aircraft, but this was a critical loss, as the glider was bearing no less a person than the commander *Leutnant* Witzig. They were well into the 49-mile climb to 8,500 feet where the towrope would be dropped, just to the northwest of the border city of Aachen, when the Ju 52 had to take sudden evasive action in the darkness to avoid collision with another faster aircraft. Pilz tried to follow, but the aircraft's sudden manoeuvre broke the towrope and the glider was flying free, well short of the point where it could conceivably reach Eben Emael.

According to Pilz, the air behind him was 'blue' as the *fallschirmjäger* and their commander gave vent to their feelings. The furious Witzig demanded to know if they would make the objective and then, showing his quick-thinking determination to reach Eben Emael, he immediately instructed Pilz to fly back to Ostheim, where he knew there were reserve Ju 52s. Turning back and following the searchlights, they spotted the Rhine below, but it was soon clear that at only 3,000 feet, they had insufficient altitude to reach their airfield. Somehow, Pilz selected a landing ground east of the Rhine, and using such height as he still had, he piloted the glider around the area, searching the darkness for signs of obstruction before putting the DFS 230 safely down in an open area.

When the aircraft had been checked over, Witzig asked Pilz if he could 'get the glider out of here'. The field was a meadow with tall grass and only a few stubby bushes and fences. Leaving Pilz, *Gefreiter* Schwarz and the four *fallschirmjäger* to clear and mark the ground, Witzig set off to Ostheim. At the double, he headed towards the nearest village where, being in *6. Armee's* concentration area, he was confident that he would find a military unit. *Leutnant* Witzig was not disappointed. He recounted:

> *I set off and began by commandeering a bicycle from a railway official, who was half asleep and just beginning his journey to the station. I promised to return the bicycle later and rode to the next village on it. There I hammered on the door of a first aid post and got the military staff doctor, still in his pyjamas, out of bed, and by threatening him with my pistol, I took his car and drove to Köln-Ostheim.*

Reaching the airfield of Ostheim shortly after 0500 hours, he found it was fast asleep and that the reserve Ju 52s had obviously returned to their own station. However, the duty officer, aware of the special nature of his station's erstwhile inhabitants of the barbed-wire fenced hangar, quickly managed to locate one of General Student's uncommitted Ju 52s at Gutersloh. But tasking a crew, checking it over and getting to the improvised landing site would take time, and by now, with the sky lightening, the rest of the *Sturmgruppe* was on its final approach to Eben Emael.

After returning to the downed DFS 230 in the Ju 52, piloted by *Feldwebel* Krutsch, with a spare set of undercarriage wheels for the takeoff, *Leutnant* Witzig recalled that

> *... the others had hastily prepared the ground by cutting down willow hedges, but we could hardly have become airborne again without the nearly indestructible Ju 52 to tow us off. In due course, I arrived at Eben-Emael, more than three hours late.*

The other section that lost its tow belonged to *Feldwebel* Maier, when for unexplained reasons the Ju 52's lights flashed, signalling the glider to release. The glider pilot *Gefreiter* Bredenbeck knew that at only 5,000 feet he was far too low, and

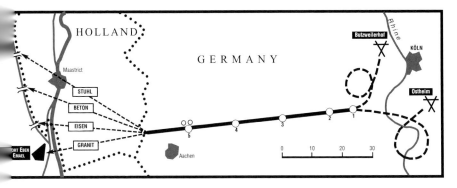

The route west from Köln was illuminated by searchlights.

it was not anywhere near time to cast off from the towrope; he was determined to hang on, but was forced to cast off when the tug banked right and went into a downward glide. Bredenbeck was not as fortunate as *Gefreiter* Pilz, and was forced to land near Duren, just over halfway to Aachen, where 2 Section joined 4th Panzer Division who were waiting to advance to the west. They crossed the Maas at Maastricht and eventually fought with 51st Pioneer Battalion on the western bank of the Albert Canal.

All was going well however for *Oberfeldwebel* Wenzel, sitting behind his pilot:

We reached Aachen, where there were three searchlights; my pilot, Brautigam, dropped the tow and the JUs turned back towards Germany, while we set course for Eben Emael.

As well as the loss of two gliders, however, and unknown to the remainder of the Sturmgruppe, *there was another problem. The tail winds were stronger than expected, which meant that some of the Ju 52s and their gliders were still below the 8,500 feet altitude required to enable the DFS 230s to glide down to their objectives, some twenty miles from the German border. With navigators making hasty calculations,* Sturmgruppe's *Concrete and Steel had to be towed over the Dutch border, thus compromising the silent approach.*

Engelmann was aboard *Oberfeldwebel* Wenzel's glider piloted by Brautigam:

Upon releasing at a height of 2600m, it was dawn, and very cold in our glider: its thin fabric skin offered us no protection from the cold. After release, the flight became smoother, and on our right we could see the lights of Maastricht. The first tracer

91

bullets appeared in the distance but none of the gliders of our sturmgruppe *was hit.*

After a gliding time of twenty minutes in which we covered 25km, we could see the outline of the fort and the Albert Canal from a height of 800 meters.

Meanwhile, with the Dutch Army by now on full invasion alert because of reports of the sound of armour manoeuvring along their border, when the noise of multiple unidentified aero engines was heard crossing from Germany, their anti-aircraft gunners opened fire.

As dawn broke, *Oberfeldwebel* Wenzel recalled that 'There was a light ground mist, through which the outlines of the fortification could be dimly perceived.' The assault was about to begin.

CHAPTER 6

THE ASSAULT

Before *Sturmabteilung* Koch had left its airfields near Köln, the Belgians were calling yet another of the general alerts that had characterised the Phoney War for the ordinary soldier. To the Belgian commanders assessing the information, this time it seemed to be the real thing. They too had detected the German panzers and vehicles moving to forward assembly areas under cover of darkness, following the issue of codeword *'Gelb'* at 2100 hours the evening before. Lower down the chain of command, however, it seemed like business as usual. *Adjutant Chef* Lambrichts described how Eben Emael's duty officer received the warning: 'It was at 0032 hours the alert order was received at the fort, emanating from Headquarters III Corps.' He recalled that the duty officer then sounded the alert via the fort's internal siren, and the process of telephoning to call in the key personnel living in the surrounding area began.

Major Jottrand was in the fort promptly, but there was little information to distinguish this alert from any of the others over the last few months. He did not immediately order the measures to bring the fort to its full defensive posture: first, demolition of the Kanne Bridge and the Lanaye Lock; second, evacuating and demolishing the barracks outside the entrance of the fort; and finally, blocking the approaches to the fort, with *Chevaux de fries*

The external barracks.

Bloc I

Cu Sud

Cupola Nord with Cupola Sud in the background.

and steel tetrahedra. Work began, however, when confirmation of the alert was received at 0300 hours (0400 German time), when troop movements on the German side of the border left no doubt as to the Germans' intentions. Just over an hour later, Major Jottrand, standing outside the entrance in Bloc 1, heard artillery fire from the direction of Maastricht, along with the sharper detonations of anti-aircraft guns. Any lingering doubt whether this was the long expected attack was gone. The process of evacuating the external barracks began, with men from the machine-gun casemates (Mi N & S) on the upper surface. They, it was assumed, would be the last into action.

Meanwhile, men in the fort's internal barracks had not been entirely convinced that this was any different from the other alerts. A young conscript Henri Lecluse recalled:

The sirens sounded in the galleries. Alert. The older soldiers were indignant at yet another exercise. I took my pyjamas off and then put them back on again. Then we heard the voices of the guard, and then the Commander in person came down the galleries and the reluctant soldiers got ready, with the exception of two older men in my room who invoked an exemption of service.

Most of the men unhurriedly made their way through the tunnels to the casemates. However, many gunners living

94

outside the fort had not been alerted: Cupola Nord (31), whose crew were to fire a blank round every thirty seconds for ten minutes, were not present, as they were among the men belatedly tasked to help demolish the barrack block. Consequently, Cupola Sud (23), whose crew was ready for action, was ordered to collect the blank rounds and fire them, but due to equipment failures, Sergeant Couclet was unable to fire them. Already, symptoms of failure to execute the fort's voluminous war plans properly and to test or at least inspect the guns properly were becoming apparent.

Eventually, Cu Sud fired the alert at around 0300 hours. Henri Lecluse wrote that 'cannon shots were fired, five in each direction plus one other'. However, as a result of the delay in firing the 'alarm gun', *Adjutant Chef* Lambrichts was one of those who, 'with an unquiet heart set out on the road to the fort, arriving at 0315 hours', some two and three quarter hours after the initial alarm. Because officers and NCOs arrived late at the fort from their houses in the surrounding villages, the process of bringing the fort to readiness for action was generally slow, and casemates were not properly crewed.

To prepare the guns for action, plugs had to be removed from the barrels and the rust-preventing cosmoline grease cleared out of the tubes and breeches. The ready stocks of 75 mm ammunition were already stored in the lower levels of the Visé and Maastricht casemates, but ammunition for the Cupolas had to be brought from the magazines in the trolleys and sent up the hoists to the room below the gun. In the case of Cupola Nord (31), which was eventually reached by its crew just before 0400 (0500) hours, the system failed. Sergeant Kipp fumed with anger and frustration, as he had no ammunition for his two 75 mm guns. The magazine that served his cupola was locked, and the NCO with the keys could not be found. When eventually the magazine was opened and the first of the 75 mm shells was loaded into the ammunition hoist, nothing happened. The power to the hoist had mysteriously failed, and the shells had to be carried up the hundred steps individually by hand. With preparations eventually complete in the casemates, the various gun crews folded down the beds mounted on the walls of the lower level of the casemates and resumed their interrupted sleep.

These early events in the fort were not considered to be

unduly important or serious at the time; being twenty miles from the German border, the garrison would have ample time to come to full operational readiness. There were after all the forward defensive belts of the Position Fortifiee de Liege (PFL) that the Germans had to break through before advancing on Eben Emael. Consequently, it was envisaged that by the time the Germans were in range of the fort, the on-duty gun crews would be manning the casemates and cupolas, while the off-duty crews from Wonk would be resting in the barracks on the lower level. The two shifts at full operational readiness would rotate on a 'hot-bed system'.

The Approach

The German account states that the Ju 52s cast off the gliders at 0410 (0510) hours. From the number of sighting reports from the various casemates, the actual time of touch down may have been earlier than planned, due to the tail winds that were stronger than anticipated. However, the fact that the gliders stood out against the lightening dawn sky to the east could account for some of the earlier reports reaching the Command Post. The DFS 230s had cast off further west than intended from their tugs over the Dutch border, and were on their fifteen-minute glide down from 8,500 feet to Eben Emael and the Albert Canal bridges. Exploding anti-aircraft shells over Maastricht rocked some of the gliders, which were flying independently rather than in a formation, but despite some near misses, the fire was ineffective. The aircraft of *Sturmabteilung* Koch glided on towards their objectives that were emerging out of the dawn. A few minutes later, having crossed the Belgian border, tracer rounds cracked through the fabric skin of the gliders. Amazingly, now at a lower level, none of the gliders was badly hit, nor were any *fallschirmjäger* soldiers wounded.

Alerted by the Dutch fire over Maastricht, Eben Emael's anti-aircraft gunners, who had reported ready at 0400 hours, peered into the sky that was beginning to lighten from the east. *Adjutant Chef* Lambrichts's report records that as the volume of anti-aircraft fire to the east increased, an 'air alert' was passed to the casemates.

Some time after 0400 hours, Belgians in Observation Post Kanne, overlooking the Albert Canal to the northwest of the fort, reported about forty or fifty 'soundless aircraft flying over

Ju 52s flying in close formation.

them at about 1500 metres'. At first some observers apparently thought that they were engined aircraft that had suffered damage and were seeking to crash-land. Shortly afterwards, Major Jottrand saw for himself the silhouette of an aircraft circling over the fort, and realised that the silent plane was manoeuvring to land on the fort. Dashing into Bloc 1, Jottrand gave orders to blow the Kanne Bridge and the Lanaye Lock.

Approaching Eben Emael, piloting Section 3, Pilot Supper had identified his landmark: the junction of the Albert Canal and the Meuse River. He flew to the south of the fort, and reported seeing Belgian troops around the entrance, some standing staring up at him.

Sturmgruppe Granit's Section 8, piloted by Diestelmeir, were in the first glider over the fort:

> *On the 10th May 1940, I came in from an easterly direction but I still had considerably more height than had been calculated beforehand. I arrived over the fort at 300 metres and there was still none of the other transport aircraft to be seen. Since I still had so much height, I pulled out the ailerons, which pressed against the machine, so that I flew in a gigantic circle at a speed of 7 metres a second but losing height.*
>
> *I was being shot at by the Belgian anti-aircraft position as we glided around the fort, but I rolled the transport glider from side to side on the approach, so that I was not a steady target and that worked quite well. I wasn't hit and my aircraft remained whole and spotless, and nobody was injured either. I landed at 0524 hours, just at daybreak.*

As the gliders manoeuvred over the fort, to his surprise,

Jottrand could not hear his anti-aircraft machine guns firing, so he telephoned *Adjutant* Longdoz, commander of the upper surface, who declared 'I'm not firing, as I can't see if they are friendly or enemy'. While the officers discussed the situation, the four anti-aircraft machine-gun crews, according to Sergeant Antoine, took action on their own initiative:

> *As the dawn began to break we could hear sounds in the air above us but no engine noise. Several gliders flew over us, so without waiting for orders our senior sergeant gave the order to open fire. Tracer flew from the five guns but it was a wasted effort.*

The machine guns had belatedly opened fire at close range, but the gliders approaching the fort from the northeast were now too close and flying too fast. It was six minutes before the German panzer spearheads were to pour over the border into Belgium and Holland.

The Landing and Attack

> '*Eben 1 here. Aircraft have landed on top of the fort!*'
>
> Report to the Command Post: 10 May 1940.

The Germans are generally quoted as having planned the time of the landing as 0425 (0525) hours. However, Belgian records indicate that reports of landings on the football pitch were reaching the Command Post at 0410 hours. Since the Belgians would have had the time and capacity to record messages accurately in signals logs, and the *fallschirmjäger* would not, the correct time for the landing of the first aircraft is probably a little before 0410 hours.

Before embarking on the detail of the attack on the fort and its defence, it is worth using *Leutnant* Witzig's own overview of the operation to set the scene:

> *Under the command of* Feldwebel *Wenzel, who took over until my arrival later, Wenzel led the seven sections totalling fifty-five men in the action, because two sections had been sent to attack the northern area, which we had assumed would be particularly strongly fortified. As it happened, these two objectives* [14 and 16] *proved to be dummy works with tin domes of a large diameter, so that the efforts of these two sections were wasted during those first decisive minutes.*
>
> *Further south in the fort, the anti-aircraft post (29) was*

Cu 120

The view across the open upper surface to CU120. This made an excellent landing zone with few obstacles, other than a pair of goal posts.

captured immediately. The occupants of the hangar offered some resistance but were soon silenced, and in the first ten minutes, the sections successfully attacked nine of the other main enemy positions, although one installation later started firing from its sunken dome. Charges were placed on seven armoured observation domes and five exploded with complete success; nine 75 mm guns in three casemates were destroyed, but the flat armoured dome 6 metres in diameter [Cu 120] was not penetrated by the 50 kilo hollow charge.

During the struggle on the surface area, we could only move under cover of fire coming from within the area of the southern corner. We came across no mines anywhere. The only instal-lations protected by barbed wire were in the north, where the sappers had to free themselves with wire cutters and turn their flamethrower on a machine gun firing from an embrasure, before they could place their charges.

Cupola Nord (31) First to land were *Feldwebel* Unger and

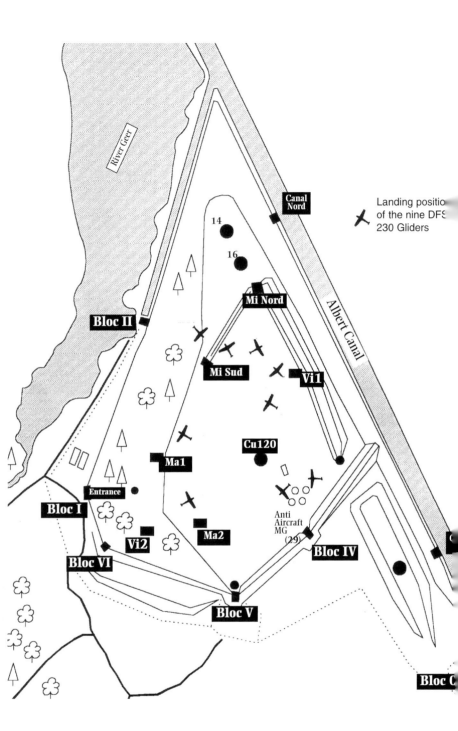

Section 8, who had been met with anti-aircraft machine gun fire as they descended steeply towards the fort, piloted by Pilot Diestelmeir. He recalled that:

> *I lost height quickly to avoid the anti-aircraft fire. Keeping low, we swung towards the south and came in from that direction to land on the surface without incident about 30 yards from our objective. Immediately after the landing, the pioneers were out of my glider at the fastest possible speed. Everyone grabbed their 25 kilos of explosive and then rushed up to the cupola.*

Inside, Sergent Joris peering through the cupola's periscope saw the gliders coming into land in the open area to his north. He lowered the retractable cupola back down into its chamber in the casemate and reported to the command post that 'Aircraft have landed near Mi Nord!'(19)

As Diestelmeir's glider came to a halt, Belgians sheltering in the hangar (25) opened fire on Section 8, and *Feldwebel* Meyer fell wounded within feet of the glider. Being the first to land and only about thirty yards from the hangar, *Feldwebel* Unger and his men had attracted most of the immediate small-arms fire.

Cupola Nord showing the lower level and the steel access door.

Weinert got himself into cover by the glider, flicked open the bipod legs of his MG 34, unlooped the belt of 7.92 mm ammunition from around the gun, and returned the fire. Under cover of the Spandau's fire, *Gefreiters* Else and Pliz dashed towards the hangar. As they approached the building, they were joined in the battle by *Feldwebel* Hauge's section, who had already captured their objective (29 – see below). Else detonated a conventional 2.5 kilo explosive charge by the door, which effectively subdued the Belgians inside. *Soldats* Remy and Heine were killed and *Adjutant* Longdoz was wounded. It is a testimony to the thoroughness of the *fallschirmjäger* that this potentially dangerous group of Belgians, led by an officer, was dealt with so promptly.

Meanwhile, *Feldwebel* Unger, assisted by Hooge and Hierlaender, ran as fast as they could towards Cupola Nord (31). Inside the cupola, Sergent Joris was shouting for his missing ammunition. If 75 mm canister rounds designed to sweep the top of the fort shot-gun style had been available at that moment, the result of the attack on Eben Emael might have been very different. At this point, however, Hanot appeared with a couple of normal HE rounds, having carried them up the stairway from the magazine. They were promptly loaded into the two breeches, but just as the cupola was about to be raised, an explosion rocked the very foundations of the concrete structure.

From his position by the glider, Diestelmeir watched Cupola Nord as:

> ...two men placed the 50 kg charge, fused and ignited it. I was lying close by and the detonation was of incredible strength, so that the whole ground shook and I was actually thrown up in the air; but with this explosion the bunker was put out of action.

Sergent Joris recalled that 'I had just come back into the cupola when there was a tremendous explosion,' which penetrated the steel of the cupola. Inside, the blast twisted the guns in their stanchions, damaged the cupola's ammunition mechanism, and cut the cables of the control system. The cupola was knocked out before it had fired a single shot.

Outside the casemate, *Feldwebel* Unger had positioned a man to cover the heavy steel door of the infantry sally port, as this was the most likely point from which they could be counter-attacked. Dealing with this was Unger's next target. Placing a 12.5 kilo hollow charge against the door, he blew it off its hinges

and caused large chunks of concrete to block the opening, sealing it against a possible Belgian counter-attack. The defenders had no intention of counter-attacking, but they did bring their machine gun into action, firing at the *fallschirmjäger* who were attacking other structures along the southern edge of the fort. A conventional 2.5 kilo explosive charge was placed under the gun's mount, but failed to stop it firing. But at 0545 hours, some 40 minutes after Sergant Joris had first seen the gliders, Major Jottrand ordered that Cupola Nord was to be abandoned.

The remains of the crew withdrew to the foot of the stairwell where they barricaded the 'airlock' doors with the pre-prepared steel beams and sand-bags.

The Anti-aircraft Position (29)

Feldwebel Haug and Section 5 were to destroy the anti-aircraft machine guns grouped together above Bloc V. Their glider was among the first aircraft to land, piloted by *Feldwebel* Heiner Lange, who recounted:

> *I was being shot at as I approached the fort by machine gun fire and it was a display of fireworks that I did not enjoy! I rolled the aircraft a bit to get through. It was strange to see tracer bullets seemingly coming straight at me, only for them to go on past at the last moment to the left and right. But they gave me an advantage, as I knew exactly where I had to go. That was where the anti-aircraft*

Top: hollow charge in its container.
Centre: Hollow charge 50 kilo.
Below: A charge explodes against a cupola.

103

The effect of a 50 kilo hollow charge on Cu Nord.

fire was coming from and that was where I had to go.
The bullets tore through the fabric and ricocheted off the steel tubing of the glider. On the ground, Sergeant Antoine recalled that 'One of the aircraft came down right in front of us and struck our gun a glancing blow, knocking it over'. Lange continued:

> *...and I came in so low that with the left wing strut I tore a machine gun out of its pit and then I halted next to another machine gun position. The crew were just standing there with the glider above them. It was an absolute egg of a landing as we glider pilots say!*

> *Then I opened the cockpit, undid my belt, climbed on to the edge of the transport glider and jumped into the shallow machine-gun pit where the four Belgian gunners were cowering. I had my pistol in my right hand and my dagger in my left. I must have made a fearful sort of impression, as they immediately put up their hands.*

Lange had in fact jumped into the machine-gun pit at the same time as *Feldwebel* Haug dropped a stick grenade into it, not realising that Lange was about to jump. Fortunately for Lange and the Belgians, the grenade did not work properly, with only the detonator functioning. Lange was understandably greatly aggrieved by this very near 'own goal'.

However, seeing that Lange had the situation under control, Haug turned his attention to another pit where three Belgians were loosing off sustained bursts of machine-gun fire at the Germans. Followed by the remainder of Section 5, he led his men forward. Two *fallschirmjäger* dashed towards the pit firing their MP 38s as they went. A stick grenade thrown in the pit exploded this time, killing one and leaving two dazed but otherwise unhurt Belgians to be taken prisoner.

With the prompt surrender of the anti-aircraft gunners, the *fallschirmjäger* of Section 5 were free to help subdue resistance in the hut, leaving Heiner Lange to deal with the Belgians. Lange told his prisoners:

> *... to get out of the pit, which they did with me following*

One of the gliders photographed on the upper surface of the fort by German Army photographers. Unlike others, this one was not released to the press.

Bloc IV with the observation bell on top. Left: The effect of a hollow charge on one of the fort's bells.

behind them. Then they were all coming towards me from the other machine-gun posts, so suddenly I had fourteen or sixteen prisoners to look after.

Bloc IV (30) *Feldwebel* Haug's Section 5 also promptly attacked the small observation bell on top of Bloc IV, which was close to the anti-aircraft machine gun pits. Inside the bell, with a restricted arc of vision, Furnelle had not seen the first gliders land, and had just called down to Simon that 'Something appears to be landing... !' when the explosion of one of Section 5's hollow charges blew him to bits. Simon was seriously wounded. The remainder of the crew of Bloc IV were deafened but able to remain at their post.

Maastricht 2 (18) This north-facing casemate, mounting three 75 mm guns and the artillery OP Eben III, was the objective of *Feldwebel* Niedermeir and his Section 1. Also aboard the glider was *Leutnant* Delica who, as the only other officer in *Sturmgruppe Granit*, was the second in command. Flown by *Feldwebel* Raschke, they made a heavy landing, due to the speed of their approach, but it was none the less accurate, in the open area between Maastricht 2 (18) and Cupola 120 (24), at 0425 hrs.

It would appear that Sergeants Marchoul and David inside the OP on top of the Ma 2 had not seen the gliders landing, and the first they knew of the attack was when they saw unfamiliar feet and legs on top of their casemate. *Sergeant* Marchoul had shouted a warning to the gun crews below that 'someone was on the casemate carrying a large item' but before he could add any more, the hollow charge detonated. The legs belonged to *Obergefreiter* Drucks and *Feldwebel* Niedermeir, and the latter recounted how he:

> *...placed the hollow charge on the OP and ignited it. Then we took cover as quickly as possible behind a bank. After about 2 or 3 seconds, the charge exploded. We jumped up and rushed back to the target to see what effect this charge had achieved. It had made a hole 6 inches wide and about 4 inches deep, so it hadn't*

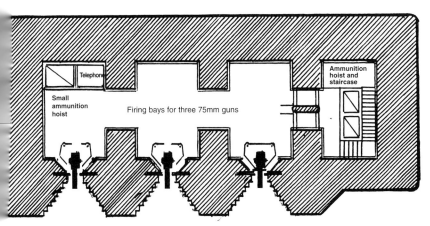

Maastricht 2 casemate.

The breech of a 75 mm gun in position in a casemate. During the attack one of these was blown off its mounting creating a hole large enough for the attackers to get inside.

gone through the cupola. We later found out that the effects on the inside were disastrous in spite of not penetrating, because the explosion had caused splinters of steel to fly off.

Both Sergeants Marchoul and David were killed. *Obergefreiters* Kramer and Graf brought up the second 12.5 kilo charge, as *Feldwebel* Niedermeir described:

'Then as we had practised, the man delegated to do so brought the second charge and placed it in the mouth of an embrasure. He

ignited it and we took cover again. After it had exploded, we jumped up again in order to see what effect it had had. We could see that the gun had been torn from its mounting and thrown inwards into the casemate and lay like a crumpled matchbox in the corner. The opening was 60 cm x 60 cm so it was big enough for anyone to climb in easily.

Inside the casemate there was of course a lot of smoke caused by the explosion, so we couldn't go straight into the room and had to wait until the smoke had dispersed and the dust settled. We had to put on our gas masks and then we climbed into the casemate. Inside we saw two dead men and one wounded.

Looking through the aperture into the dust-laden but still electrically illuminated interior, the Germans could see bodies lying amongst the wreckage. Belgian conscripts Philippe and Ferrire lay dead and *Caporal* Verbois was mortally wounded. The other gunners, who had been thrown from their positions against the casemate's concrete walls, lay wounded: burned or simply stunned by the blast and smoke. The casemate's two signallers were missing. As the wounded were dragged down from the shambles of the casemate to the lower level, a 3 kilo charge exploded in the barrel of Gun Number Two.

There was a further detonation as Sergeant Poncelet ordered his Belgian gunners to withdraw down the steel stairway from Ma 2. On their way down the stairs, there was the rattle of machine-gun fire above them, as *Feldwebel* Niedermeier and two of his soldiers, wearing their gas masks against the dust and fumes, climbed in to the vacated casemate. The *fallschirmjäger* fired several *Schmeiser* bursts down the stairwell to hurry the Belgians on their way.

Having reached the tunnels of the Intermediate Level, Sergeant Poncelet instructed the shocked gunners to seal the access to the casemate. With the sound of the Germans in the casemate above them, they justifiably feared that the enemy would follow them into the heart of the fort. The steel beams were fitted into their channels and sandbags were packed into the small chamber between the pair of steel doors. Meanwhile, the Germans carried the dying *Caporal* Verbois out of the casemate through the gap where the 75 mm had been blown off its mounting, and unable to treat him, laid him on a bank where he died shortly afterwards.

Within the first minutes of the assault on Eben Emael, a

Fallschirmjäger, some of them wounded, guard Belgian prisoners.

second 'offensive' casemate was knocked out, and of the remaining five artillery cupolas and casemates, three were under attack. The remaining two had probably not been properly identified by German intelligence, which in itself tends to confirm that at least some of the conspiracy theories are exaggerated.

As planned, *Feldwebel* Niedermeier sent Drucks to the north across the open area of the fort to find *Leutnant* Witzig and to report success at objective 18 (Ma 2). While the *fallschirmjäger* sections were attacking the casemates and reorganising, the pilots who were not herding prisoners of war laid out aircraft identification panels alongside the captured casemates. These were signals for the Stukas, which were on call to support *Sturmgruppe Granit* should they fail to knock out specific casemates.

Maastricht 1 (12) Ma 1 was the objective of *Feldwebel* Arent's Section 3. They had come under machine-gun fire at about 100 feet while Chief Pilot Supper was on his landing approach to the fort, but a banking dive brought the glider down safely. Skidding to a halt some twenty-five yards east of their objective, Arent was first out of the aircraft, urging on his men who were struggling with their cumbersome sections of the charges.

A search for an access door into the casemate, which was to be blown in order to prevent the Belgian garrison from launching a counter-attack, was fruitless. The silent and sightless casemate (there was no observation cupola Ma 1) presented a quandary, as there was no obvious way of neutralising it, other than blowing in the gun embrasure. This they elected to attempt with their 50 kilo hollow charge, but there was no convenient surface on which to mount the bulky charge. Consequently, they abandoned

Feldwebel **Peter Arent.**

the larger version, and managed to wedge the smaller 12.5 kilo charge above the steel sponson that held the 75 mm gun. Igniting the fuse, Arent ran for cover. However, possibly over-familiar from training with the charges, Arent and his men were too close to the casemate when the charge detonated, having turned around to see it in action for real. Knocked flat and stunned by the explosion, it was some moments before the *fallschirmjäger* returned to examine their target, which now had a hole less than two feet square blown through the concrete and steel, out of which were pouring oily clouds of smoke. Through the hole, they could hear the moans of the wounded Belgian gun crew who were just regaining consciousness amidst the smouldering propellant charges ignited in their cart by the

Maastricht 1. Arent's charge blew a hole in the left embrasure.

German *fallschirmjäger* firing a *Schmeiser*.

explosion of the hollow charge.

Inside the Ma 1 there was chaos. The blast had thrown Belgian gunner Langelen from his position beside the 75 mm gun into the telephone room, while the gun itself had been torn from its mount and thrown around the casemate, crushing Private Borman against the chamber's ventilator, before falling into the stairwell where it came to rest. A shaft of daylight billowing with clouds of dust and smoke penetrated the darkness where Sergeant Gigon, badly concussed, located two of his wounded soldiers from their moans and carried them to the casemate's lower level. Sergeant Gigon retuned for a third trip to the gun room, but the 75 mm propellant charges were now burning vigorously, producing a smoke that was so thick that his gas mask was more of a hindrance than a help. The smoke and the rattle of *Schmeiser* fire and the 9 mm Parabellum bullets ricocheting off the concrete walls drove Sergeant Gigon back to the stairwell. Staggering to the lower level, he fell into the arms of one of his men. Before being taken down to the fort's hospital, he reported to Lieutenant Deuse, who was gathering his gunners for a counter-attack on the casemate's Upper Level, that there were still wounded men up in the gun room. However, the Belgians could now hear enemy activity in the chamber above them.

Feldwebel Arent had climbed feet first through the small hole he had blown in the embrasure; feeling his way through the smoke-filled space, he made his way to the sound of a moaning Belgian gunner, who was barely conscious but not severely wounded. Dragging his prisoner to the hole, Arent handed him over to Kupsch and Stopp, who had also climbed into the casemate. Two more Belgians, one of whom had gunshot wounds, were located and taken out through the hole. At this stage, *Feldwebel* Arent heard the sounds of Lieutenant Deuse's counter-attack forming up below. To deter them, he dropped a 2.5 kilo charge down the shaft, but in the confined space the

Mi Sud showing 1940 battle damage to the main embrasure, now blocked with concrete.

Fallschirmjäger pioneers pictured using a classic German assault weapon – the *flammenwaffer*.

resulting explosion was so severe that it stunned the Germans, who were thrown against the casemate's concrete wall. However, there was silence below and the glow of lights had gone out.

Feldwebel Arent's next task was to destroy the generator plant's armoured exhaust tower and to deal with Bloc II, but these were low priorities, as they were not a part of the fort's offensive armament.

Mi Sud (13) Chief Pilot Schultz piloted Section 9's DFS 230 to a landing about fifty yards east of their objective, one of the two machine gun casemates, whose three embrasures presented an immediate threat to the *fallschirmjäger* moving around on the fort's open upper surface. Because the crews of casemates Mi Sud and Mi Nord were expected to be the last to be in action (only needed after a considerable period of time, once the enemy had closed in on the fort via Maastricht), the machine gunners had been detailed to move documents, etc. into the fort and destroy the external barrack blocks. Consequently, the casemates that could have made all the difference were unmanned at the vital moment when the gliders landed and the *fallschirmjäger* would have been relatively easy targets. The Germans could not possibly have planned for this eventuality, so this is an example of luck in war, or perhaps the way daring innovation produces surprise that in turn affects the outcome of a battle.

Unlike the defences around the southern artillery and the anti-aircraft casemates, barbed-wire entanglements surrounded Mi Sud. *Feldwebel* Neuhaus did not have an easy time as he came under fire from the fort's other Belgian positions, including, initially, from the area of the hanger, while he cut his way through the barbed wire. There was inevitable delay as wire snagged the clothing of both Neuhaus and his men who were following through the gap with the hollow charges and a flamethrower. So intense was the fire from the south that the *fallschirmjäger* were temporarily driven into the cover on the northern side of the earth bank. With Adjutant Longdoz and his men in the hanger dealt with, *Feldwebel* Neuhaus and two of his men were able to crawl around the area of the casemate.

By now, the Belgians had belatedly occupied Mi Sud, and its south-facing machine gun had come into action. Avoiding the field of fire, Schlosser moved into a position from where he could use his flame-thrower against the embrasure. The lance of black smoking fire silenced the Belgian machine gunners, giving an opportunity for the German pioneers to quickly place a 12.5 kilo hollow charge in the machine gun embrasure, light the fuse, and retire. However, the Belgian crew had probably seen the goings-on in front of the embrasure through their sight opening. Opening the breech of their gun, the Belgians pushed the precariously wedged charge off the embrasure with a cleaning rod they pushed up the gun's bore. The charge fell to the ground where it exploded ineffectually, but with two further 12.5 kilo and three 50 kilo charges, the south-facing embrasure was soon blown in and the observation bell penetrated by a 50 kilo hollow charge. *Feldwebel* Neuhaus now turned his attention to the casemate's steel sally-port door, which he attacked with another 50 kilo charge. The explosion not only blew in the door into the casemate, but the frame as well. At this point, having only been in their positions for a matter of moments, the shaken Belgians withdrew to the Intermediate Level. First throwing grenades into the structure to make sure it was clear, the Germans entered Mi Sud, where they found several stunned Belgians who had been left behind during the withdrawal. *Feldwebel* Neuhaus did not follow the Belgians down into the fort, as his secondary task was to help give covering fire to the sections clearing the northern part of the fort. He sited his men in fire positions both inside the casemate and outside along the east slope. As it was

Barbed wire and gliders in the area of the machine gun casemate.

The only remaining false cupola, now on display outside the fort's main entrance.

apparent that there was no immediate threat from the north, Section 9's runner set off to *Leutnant* Witzig to report that Mi Sud had been captured, and that he was awaiting further tasks.

The Northern False Cupolas (14 and 16)   Assessed by German intelligence as two of Eben Emael's most powerful positions, the fake 120 mm cupolas sited in the northern apex of the fort were each allocated a valuable section of Witzig's *Sturmgruppe*. Landing northeast and northwest of Mi Sud (13), the sections were 150 to 175 yards from their objectives. *Feldwebels* Harlos and Heinemann led their men forward to their objectives, using Bangalore Torpedoes to blast their way through the barbed wire in this area, only to find that the cupola were light metal decoys. The combat power of two valuable sections had been distracted from attacking the fort's main offensive batteries by one of the oldest but none the less effective *ruses de guerre*. The Germans had also identified a cupola beyond the Fort's southern boundary (32). This too was a false position, but the Germans had either identified this as such or had realised that this position was beyond their capacity to attack, because it was ignored by the *fallschirmjäger*.

See map page 100

Mi Nord (19)   There was no deception in Mi Nord. This key position was sited to cover the fort's open upper area, and was capable of bringing down lethal machine gun fire on the southern casemates, where the bulk of *Sturmgruppe* Granit were fighting. Kurt Engelmann was one of Section 4's soldiers, who

116

described Mi Nord:

> Our objective was equipped with 3 heavy machine guns, 2 armoured searchlights, 1 artillery observation cupola and 1 light machine-gun to cover the entrance.

Somewhat before 0430 (0530) hours, two Belgian NCOs Vossen and Bataille had just occupied the Eben II OP on top of Mi Nord, and were heard talking about aeroplanes and men running around on the surface. Before they could say more there was a shattering explosion. Their attacker *Feldwebel* Wenzel recounted:

> On landing, I ran immediately to the bunker that I was to attack, and up the earth bank to the right, on to the roof. I saw that the cupola had a hole in the top – the periscope hole. I had a 1 kilo charge with me, ignition time four seconds, so I pulled it off and counted to two and only then did I drop it through the opening into the casemate. Before the explosion, I could hear running

A *fallschirmjäger* shelters from the explosion of a 12.5 kilo hollow charge.

The open ground in front of Mi Nord where Wenzel's glider landed.

Eben II Op

Wenzel's route

Mi Nord photograph taken after the attack. Note the barbed wire stanchions.

> feet inside; afterwards it was all quiet. But, meanwhile, my
> section had arrived with the 50 kilo charge. We put it straight on
> top of the cupola and lit it.

Both of the Belgian NCOs in the observation post had been killed. A 12.5 kilo charge blew in the south-facing machine gun embrasure, but the opening was too small for the Germans to use as an entrance, so *Feldwebel* Wenzel ordered his men to use a second and larger 50 kilo charge. Engelmann was one of those carrying the unused charge:

> In the meantime, the rest of our Truppe had taken up position
> in the bushes in front of the rampart, and our machine gunner,

Mi Nord after the attack.

Eben II Op

Polzin, took the casemate openings under fire. I and another man each took half of another 50 kilo pack and rushed toward the bunker. This charge was suspended and ignited in front of a machine gun embrasure. We threw ourselves behind a rampart four metres away, but we still felt the enormous shock wave when it detonated. The charge blew a very big hole into the concrete wall of the casemate, so that an entry into the bunker was now possible. An awful view awaited us when we entered the casemate.

After the detonation, *Feldwebel* Wenzel was again at the forefront of the action:

Straight after the explosion I was in there. Everything was full of smoke and it was dark but with the help of a torch, I could feel my way around. In the first room, I saw the Belgian machine gun crew. They were all fallen – dead. Then as I felt my way further into the room at the back, suddenly the telephone rang behind me and I have to say that its unexpected ring was the first time I had been shaken at Eben Emael! I turned round and with my torch felt my way along and found the telephone in a niche in the wall. I picked up the receiver and at the other end, I heard a terribly agitated voice speaking French. I didn't understand any French and so I waited until there was a pause then I said quite calmly but emphatically "Here are the Germans!" To that came the answer: "Oh mon Dieu!"

Engelmann recalled that once Mi Nord (19) had been taken:

Casemate 19 had been destroyed and was no longer able to offer any resistance, our Truppe had accomplished its mission within fifteen minutes of landing on the fort. We proceeded to drape a flag on the bunker as a marker for the Luftwaffe to indicate that the casemate was in our hands. Now we had time to take a closer look at our surroundings. The detonations from the other positions had almost ceased by this time.

Artillery observation officer Leutnant Delica.

Our Truppeführer, Feldwebel *Wenzel, then set up his command post against the rampart next to Casemate 19 [Mi Nord] and put the seven of us into a defensive position. This location was chosen for the command post because of its excellent observation of the entire fort, with the exception of the southern and western positions, which were located on slopes and could not be seen due to thickets.*

Feldwebel Wenzel, with the bandaged head, and the survivors of his section after the battle.

> *Wenzel himself went around the nearby casemates to find out which of them had not yet been destroyed, and at the same time, find our* Sturmgruppe *Leader* Leutnant *Witzig, and report the capture of Casemate 19* [Mi Nord]. *On the way, he met our radio operator, Gilg, who was also looking for Witzig to receive orders to set up the radio post. None of the other runners who had been sent out to find Witzig or members of Truppe 11 had been successful. Wenzel concluded that Truppe 11 had not landed on the fort.*

Wenzel ordered the radio operators to signal *Hauptmann* Koch at the Albert Canal bridges with the message 'Objective achieved, everything in order'.

With the non-arrival of Witzig and with *Leutnant* Delica embroiled in the fighting that could be plainly heard still going on around Ma 2, *Feldwebel* Wenzel found himself in *de facto* command. Knowing the plan thoroughly, he was able to fulfil this function admirably until Witzig arrived three hours later. Wenzel later commented, 'We were so well trained that we did not need the officers.' Engelmann continued his account:

Wenzel decided to act, and he took command himself. He had the radio team set up their position at the northern rampart and established the dressing post there, as the initial fighting had already cost two dead and twelve wounded.

Wenzel arranged for radio contact to be established with Sturmgruppe Beton [Concrete] at Vroenhoeven, where Hauptmann Koch had his command post. He managed to give his situation report and also called up Stuka support to suppress the positions around the fort's entrance and to prevent supplies being brought up from the village of Eben Emael. Within twenty minutes, Ju 87 [Stukas] and HS 126 aircraft appeared and put on a show of precision bombing. One He 111 [Heinkel bomber] flew over the fort and dropped containers filled with fresh ammunition.

Cupola 120 (24) In the centre of the open area were the fort's most potent weapons, the twin 120 mm guns mounted in a large revolving steel cupola that looked similar to the fake cupolas (14 and 16) that had already been attacked on the northern part of the fort's Upper Surface. *Feldwebel* Max Maier's Section 2 was to attack Cu 120, but their glider, it will be recalled, had failed to reach the fort when it dropped its tow. Consequently, this

Present-day visitors to Eben Emael viewing the breech traversing mechanism and one of the guns inside Cu 120.

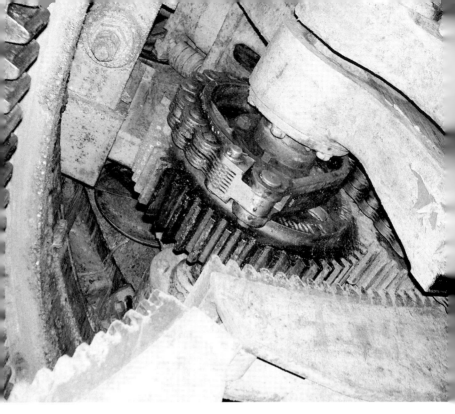

A part of the complicated traversing and elevating mechanism of Cu 120.

120 mm ammunition carts for bringing up ammunition from the magazine on the Intermediate Level.

cupola was not neutralised in the first wave of attacks. Potentially, this was an extremely dangerous failure, as the Panzer spearheads would soon be within range of the 120 mm guns.

Inside the steel cupola, Sergeant Rene Cremer was watching through his gun sight the gliders skidding to a halt around him, and listening to the repeated heavy detonations of the hollow charges on the surrounding casemates. However, his view was not good, as he later reported:

My field of observation was restricted due to the absence of the periscope. I had to slowly traverse the whole cupola to be able to see the whole area of the superstructure.

Without the benefit of a periscope that could be quickly rotated, which should have been fitted to the cupola, the one man who was in a position to report accurately was only able to pass the sketchiest of details, despite the demands of the command post. Cremer continues:

I saw a group of these sons of the devil under the wing of their glider, situated midway between my casemate and Cupola Nord. I communicated my observations immediately to Command Post and asked permission to act as quickly as possible.

At last, an order to shoot comes through: Fire on the hill in front of Bloc I, with shells that have fuses set to burst the shell in the shortest possible time. I immediately give my orders, and the factory that is the cupola starts moving. The munitions are placed in the hoist and then the first incident: the hoists are not working. Then the second incident: the ammunition loader prepares his equipment and sees that the shafts of the pincers have disappeared, and I immediately send a man to the repair workshop, and while waiting, we fix the hoist and unpack the ammunition to load the guns.

Cremer informed the command that the hoist was not working, and that his men without the pincers were breaking open the boxes by hand, using their pocket knives and hammers. Finally, some ammunition fused for clearing the upper surface was unpacked and carried up to the guns.

I aim my cupola by looking through the barrel of one of the guns, but it's with a heavy heart that I realise that my line of vision passes far above Cupola Nord: too bad, I say, I'm going to fire like that anyway.

The third incident was that there's no way to separate the two pieces of the counterweight [in the turret mechanism]. *It's my corporal van Gelooven who shouts this information to me. I task Gysens and Malchair to observe through the sight's telescope in the dugout, and rush to the Intermediate Level. Everything seems OK, but the counterweight doesn't fall, the clutch won't open, and in spite of all my attempts, I can't separate them. So I decide to operate the loading mechanism by hand, but whether the shell is too heavy or the manual pressure of the rammer is not strong enough, the shell doesn't load and the mechanism falls back again each time. Leaving the corporal to continue the work, I'm sure he is capable but he is convinced that he won't be able to fix the mechanism. I didn't think he could either, even though he had a deep understanding of equipment.*

Without being attacked, Cupola 120 (24) was out of action, while the Belgian gunners struggled to repair the mechanism. In 1960, during one of Colonel Mrazek's visits to the fort, Rene Cremer described the incidents that rendered Cu 120 inoperable. 'His voice carried a note of bitterness. I remarked that it was rumoured that there may have been treachery behind these occurrences. He shrugged his shoulders and laconically said, *"peut-être."* [perhaps].'

Visé 1 (26) Set into the large bank of earth on the fort's eastern edge, Vi 1 was sited to engage targets to the south, and the crew consequently had a good view of the events on the southern edge of the fort. This casemate was also to have been attacked by *Feldwebel* Maier's missing Section 2. However, *Feldwebel*

The south facing Visé 1 casemate.

Stuka dive bombers were on call above Eben Emael throughout much of the battle.

Hubel and Section 10 had landed less than a hundred yards to the south of Vi 1. While making his way to Mi Nord, where his section was to become a part of *Granit's* reserve, Hubel realised that the casemate had not been attacked and set about dealing with it.

Meanwhile, at 0435 hours, the Belgian gun crews had been given the 'general order to fire some salvos'. However, the attacks by Stukas' drove the Belgians down to the Intermediate Level, and the detonation of 'hollow charges', blew air-intake valves off the interior of the casemate. As the Belgian gunners were unable to do anything about this attack, their morale was undermined. A little later, however, the men were back at their posts in the Vi 1 casemate:

0500: Sous Lieutenant Desloover and Mdlis Delcourt fire salvos; the officer is recalled to command post; the crew evacuate towards the Intermediate Level.

0510: Major Jottrand orders general fire "to occupy the crew" but does not have them fire on the fallschirmjäger, *as the shells pass over their heads.'*

The situation in Visé 1 was unclear, and at 0540 hours, the Command Post prematurely reported to RFL that the casemate

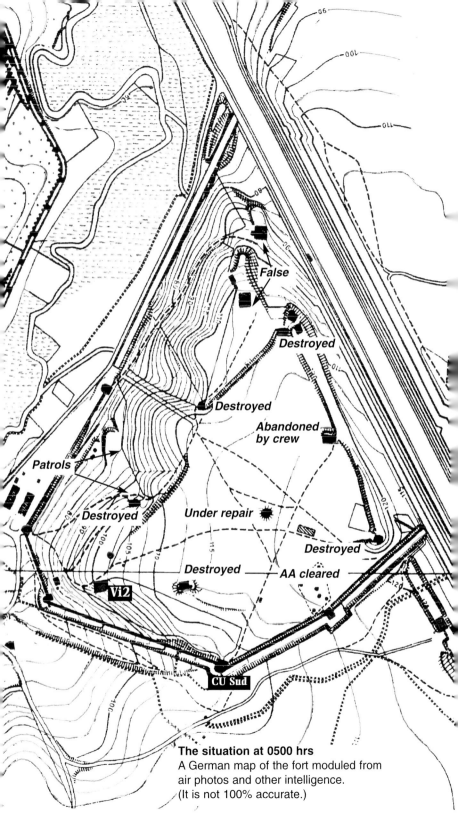

The situation at 0500 hrs
A German map of the fort moduled from
air photos and other intelligence.
(It is not 100% accurate.)

had been knocked out by the Germans. However, five minutes later, the unsettled crew, who had by now heard of the fate of the other casemates, reported 'direct hits by bombs on the casemate, and noises made by the *fallschirmjäger* coming from the exterior of the casemate'. At 0600 hours, following lack of ventilation, the crew withdrew again to the Intermediate Level.

Of *Sturmgruppe Granit's* ten initial objectives, two had proved to be dummies, the anti-aircraft machine gun positions were destroyed, and six casemates were neutralised. Cupola 120 was yet to be attacked, along with Visé 2 and Cupola Sud, both in the southeast portion of the fort.

The Situation at 0500 Hours
In Major Jottrand's Command Post, it was now abundantly clear that Germans had landed in gliders on the fort's Upper Surface. The sound of heavy detonations echoing along the corridors of the Intermediate Level and the resulting blasts of air left the officers in no doubt that the casemates and cupolas were being attacked. Information came in by telephone and runner that already the two Maastricht Battery casemates had been knocked out, along with Cupola Nord, the anti-aircraft battery and the two machine-gun casemates. In addition, there was no word from Adjutant Longdoz, who had last reported being at the hanger.

To gain a clearer picture of what was happening on the Upper Surface, Major Jottrand instructed the observer in Bloc 01 (34), at the southern extremity of the fort, to leave his position, braving the Stukas circling above, and to report what the Germans were up to.

However, Major Jottrand did not wait for full information, and promptly ordered Sous Lieutenant Verstraeten to take about a dozen men from Blocs I and II and climb up the eastern slope. This patrol saw at least one of the *fallschirmjäger* on the roof of Bloc II setting up a hollow charge, but he ran, having set off the charge before the Belgians could open fire. The patrol was quickly driven back by Stukas. At *Feldwebel* Wenzel's request, passed over the radio, the aircraft were beginning to dive-bomb the casemates and cupolas that did not have the swastika air identification panels on display. Reputedly, Major Jottrand was furious and ordered Verstraeten out again, but once in the safety of the fort, the patrol had dispersed.

With the enemy on the fort's Upper Surface, and his men in the cover of concrete, Major Jottrand requested artillery fire from Headquarters PFL. During the course of 10/11 May 1940, 105 mm guns of Forts Pontisse and Barachon fired about 1,200 rounds at the Fort Eben Emael. As the shells began to land, *Feldwebel* Unger, who had completed his task in the area of Cu Nord (31), saw someone, presumably Wenzel or one of his men, signalling him to move to join him at Mi Nord (19). Unger ordered his section to disperse into an open formation to minimise casualties from the fire, but while they made their way through the scrub on the crest of the *Tranchée de Caester*, *Feldwebel* Unger was killed by a shell splinter. Only *Obergefreiter* Else and two other *fallschirmjäger* eventually joined Wenzel at his command post. Up to this point, *Sturmgruppe Granit's* casualties had been remarkably light. Other sections that had managed to blast their way into the casemates were in very good cover from Belgian fire but they too had to leave cover to complete the neutralisation of the fort's offensive capability or simply to head towards Mi Nord where they would form a defensive position.

Cupola 120 (24)   Also amongst those wounded by the shelling was glider pilot Heiner Lange, who was escorting his prisoners north from the anti-aircraft positions (29). Despite diving for cover as a salvo of 105 mm rounds impacted, he was hit by fragments from a near miss that left him with eight painful wounds. As he lay on the ground to the south of Cu 120, which was rotating as the crew sought to see what was happening, every time the cupola stopped rotating facing in his direction, Lange thought he was likely to become a target. However, the

A photograph of Cu 120 after the attack.

Belgian gunners did not fire. Lange could not know of the technical problems that the gun crew were experiencing, and with prisoners around him he was unlikely to become a target of the Cupola's main armament.

Inside, Sergeant Rene Cremer was still struggling with the loading mechanism:

I go up again immediately to the firing level, as a movement of the enemy had just been announced alongside the cupola. All at once, I see enemy movement – several of them moving towards the ramparts of our anti-aircraft machine gun positions – and under the threat of their arms, they make the men of Adjutant Longdoz, who is wounded, come out with them. I found out afterwards that the position had been attacked by grenade and machine gun. When all those machine gun crews had left their ramparts, the Germans made them march with their hands up, and placing themselves behind this living shield, progressed towards my cupola. I immediately told the gun position officer in the Command Post, who replied, "Defend yourselves as you can." I ordered the gun breeches closed [to stop grenades being dropped in] *and the cannons elevated, then with a rifle pushed into the telescope housing, I set about shooting down as many* [Germans] *as I could. I noticed that the first enemy was away from a group of Belgians, and as the chance came, I aimed and pressed the trigger. I saw my German throw his arms apart and fall face down. The others didn't even stop, and on the contrary hid themselves even more behind our men. I had just shot down my first enemy, which encouraged me, along with*

Artist's impression of the attack on Cu 120. *David Wright*

my men who had given a great shout when I hit my target.

Recovering from the immediate shock of his shell-splinter wounds, Lange decided to deal with the rotating cupola that was now firing 7.92 mm bullets rather than 120 mm shells. He

The scar created by the explosion, was filled and painted over by the Germans, to hide the secret of the existence of the hollow charge from parties that were shown around by the proud conquerors during the following months. The original muzzle covers were blown off by the detonation.

limped back to his glider:

> ... where I knew there were plenty of explosives that had not been used by my fallschirmjäger. Despite my wounds, I knew my duty was to take action. While the turret was facing to the north, where Wenzel was, I dragged both parts of the charge up to the guns. My muscles screamed with pain and blood flowed but I reached my objective and carried the charge up onto the steel. I had seen the charges and knew how to use them. Igniting the fuse, I came down from the steel but I couldn't move very fast and there was no cover, so I was caught by the explosion.

This burst Lange's eardrums. Inside the cupola was *Sergeant* Cremer, who reported that:

> *Alas, the reply* [to my rifle shooting] *wasn't slow in coming. There was a terrible explosion on the cupola a few seconds afterwards: everything turned upside down pell-mell, men, shells, cartridge cases and equipment. A man cried out that he was wounded and the air became unbreathable, resulting in a*

precipitous and tumbling retreat down the ladders. There was a second explosion, and flames surged from top to bottom of the cupola, sounds of clashing metal in the Intermediate and Upper Levels; worse, there was no light. Believing that the cupola was gutted, and myself suffocating, I went down into the gallery and had a barrier of small beams made at the foot of the work.

It all had a terrible effect on morale, and we were all shattered. A man complained his leg hurt, so I sent him to the infirmary. Luckily, there were no men wounded. Commandant *van der Auwera paid us a visit, and speaking about the situation, easily managed to raise my mens' morale, and the cupola was soon reoccupied.*

Artillery Support

The picture was not entirely bleak for the Belgians, as the fort was still able to carry out a number of artillery-fire missions in support of surrounding formations and units, despite the under-manning of the surviving casemates and sundry technical problems. The guns in action were mainly from casemates whose offensive function had not been properly identified, or, as in the case of the genuine Cu 120, had not been attacked. The fire in a northerly direction was in response to calls from 7th Infantry Division's observers manning the Position Fortifiee de Liege, while the lesser volume to the north was directed on the line of the Albert Canal, where the bridges were under attack. It is variously estimated that between 1,000 and 3,000 rounds of 75 mm ammunition were fired. With the fort's guns in action, *Sturmgruppe Granit* had not yet completely succeeded in their mission. To claim that the *fallschirmjäger* had 'achieved their objective within an hour' is a clear overstatement that has its origins in German wartime propaganda.

Cupola Sud (23) This cupola was sited above Bloc V at the southern extremity of the fort and was not planned to be attacked in the initial assault. There are various theories regarding this omission in the German plan. The most credible explanation is that intelligence on the fort's upper surface, developed mainly from high level air photographs, had failed to identify the exact nature of the cupola. Unlike Cupola Nord that had been quickly knocked out, Cupola Sud was in action, as

Cupola Sud elevated to the firing position.

ordered by the Command Post, in support of 7th Infantry Division who were holding the Albert Canal bridges to the north and firing in self defence. Short of manpower, some of the gun crew under *Mdlis* Hanot were sent to Cupola Sud from Cupola Nord, to make up numbers, but it was soon apparent that the survivors were so badly shaken that 'they were practically useless'. In addition it is recorded that:

> *Re-supply was almost impossible, as a kind of panic reigned in the underground barracks, where some men suggested that the Germans occupied several of the cupolas and blocs as well as certain tunnels, and that this presented too much risk for the supply teams.*

Despite the rumours and shortages of ammunition at the Cupola later in the battle, the gun crew of Cu Sud resolutely continued to serve their guns in the best tradition of their arm of the Service.

Visé 2 (9) Visé 2, in the southeast corner of the fort, was also not attacked by *Sturmgruppe* Witzig in the first hour, as the guns faced south and could not threaten the Germans in the centre of the Upper Surface. However, the sound of battle was only too obvious to the gun crews, including Henri Lecluse, who, unaware of the enemy's success at this early stage, reported that there was:

> *...a boom of great calibre shell falling near our casemate* [probably a hollow charge at another casemate]. *However, it only shook the work, but things were getting serious. Though overall, we felt that we were going to be able to defend ourselves*

The breech of one of the 75 mm guns inside Visé 2 (9).

An exterior view of one of the south facing embrasures of Visé 2.

and be able to fire at the enemy.

Another Belgian reported that: 'we learned by telephone that aeroplanes had landed on the surface of the fort. The lookouts spoke of about twenty unknown planes circling in the gloom. In a few minutes some terrifying explosions occurred'. Henri Lecluse recalled that a little later:

> ... *a great blast of air almost knocked us over. The old boys said that it was Cu 120 that had just fired, but I believed that a shot could not produce such a displacement of air. We received the order to open the ammunition crates. I had seen them sealed during training and now I was to see them for real. Out of one wooden zinc-lined crate came six shells, yellow with brass cases, while another soldier opened a case of fuses.*
>
> *We abandoned our* bonnet d'police [side hats] *and put on our helmets, then awaited the order to fire. At 0430 hours, the command that we had been waiting for was given; general attack fire. The ventilator was turned on and we opened the breech to load the shells. We fired type 1900.15 shells with a small charge because our target was the defence of the bloc below us.*

None of the gun crew had a well-defined job; I set the fuses, and with my feet I kicked the empty cases down into the empty case chamber where they landed with a dull thud. With the noise of the ventilator, the firing, the orders, and the clang of the empty cases on the concrete, there was a real ruckus. The firing and the orders were quite methodical, in spite of the lack of personnel required to fulfil several roles, but spirits were not frayed and the men performed their tasks as if on an exercise. The engagement lasted 25 minutes and we fired 480 rounds. The casemate was full of a dense and acrid smoke that the ventilator had difficulty in dissipating.

During Visé 2's first engagement, one of the three 75 mm-gun's firing pins broke, and as this eventuality had not been anticipated, there was no replacement available in the casemate. However, the gunners improvised and replaced the firing pin with a piece of steel wire. Henri Lecluse also recorded that not all the gunners were familiar with their task and that 'one of us dropped a fused shell without accident'. At about this time, Lecluse was forced to go down to a lower level. 'I don't know why the gas alert was given; I took off my glasses to put on my mask but it was at this moment I dropped my glasses. Being useless without my glasses, I asked to go down to repair them.' This revealing account describes what it was like for the ordinary soldier to be in the fort during the morning of 10 May 1940.

As soon as I descended to the Visé 2 magazine on the Intermediate Level I set to work with the others. The first-line ammunition that had already been in the casemate was fired during the first engagement and needed replacing. I had never been in the magazine so I was surprised.

We loaded shells into the ammunition trolley, but we lacked tools to open the boxes, so we had to cut the leather straps and scrape off the protective grease with a miniscule penknife. The laden trolleys were manoeuvrable but heavy, and the electric hoist would not stop at the right height, which made our task difficult. Instructions for the ammunition that we were to prepare were given by loudspeaker.

Summary
Fort Eben Emael's capacity to support the PFL's positions along a critical length of the Albert Canal had been largely neutralised

within fifty minutes of the surprise landing on top of the fort. The combination of gliders and explosives had worked. However, the case for the effects of the hollow charges is debatable: there are strong advocates for the German view that they had worked as intended, and also for the Belgians, who point out that in many cases it was conventional charges that had knocked out the guns. It is fair to say that the observation cupolas and bells had been effectively attacked by hollow charges, and a combination of surprise attack and the massive explosions had undermined the Belgian gun-crews' morale, which added to the physical damage caused to the casemates. Also, in some cases, the hollow charges had been used more as very large conventional charges. It was in the German interest to talk up the success of their weapons for propaganda purposes, once the secret of the hollow charge was out.

Although the Belgian garrison's morale had not been particularly good before the battle, a significant number of men were prepared to fight bravely, and most of the remainder, against a well-trained elite force who had surprised them, did their duty.

Chapter 7

HOLDING THEIR GAINS

Neutralising Eben Emael's offensive capability was the easy part of the operation. Seventy *fallschirmjäger* had landed on top of a fort whose garrison numbered almost 1,000 men, some twenty miles behind enemy lines in the midst of a major Belgian defensive belt. Survival would in many respects be a battle of wills, but the small German force was about to receive an important psychological boost.

Witzig's Return

After a spare Ju 52 that he had fetched from his original airfield towed him off in his glider from a field to the west of Köln, *Leutnant* Witzig eventually arrived over the fort 0800 (0900) hours. Wenzel and his men were initially puzzled to see another glider over the fort, but they had underestimated the determination of their commander. The glider swept in miraculously without being hit and skidded to a halt near Mi Nord (19). Witzig recounted that,

> After our landing, I went straight to our intended CP at construction 19 [Mi Nord], *which had quite clearly been taken by* Feldwebel *Wenzel. I could see the holes made by the explosion. On my arrival, Wenzel immediately reported all that had happened up until that time. And there was quite a lot to tell! As far as he could say at this stage, most of the sections had achieved their goals.*

After reviewing the situation, and with the majority of the fort's offensive capability neutralised, Witzig's main problems were to prevent the Belgians from bringing the guns in the casemates

Oberleutnant Witzig.

and cupolas back into action, and, as a very small force, to survive until 4th Panzer Division arrived to complete the capture of the fort. This was scheduled for 1000 (1100) hours, but Witzig already knew from 'sitreps' passed by *Hauptmann* Koch's radio operator that the relief force was hours behind schedule, as a result of blown bridges. If he and his men were to succeed, the Pioneer commander knew that he must repel enemy attacks

137

on his positions mainly in the northern part of the fort, and he would somehow have to carry the battle to the enemy. His first priority was dealing with the enemy that he knew to be active on the fort's western slope.

Counter-Attacks

The earlier probe by a dozen or so men led by a junior officer from Blocs I and II had failed, but at 0800 hours, Major Jottrand ordered *Sous Lieutenants* Verstraeten and Deuse out again with the same mission as before. This time, they were recalled to lead a platoon of forty men from the 2nd Grenadiers. These troops, who had only been in the area for a matter of days due to a hand-over between 5th and 7th Infantry Divisions, lacked all but the most rudimentary knowledge of the layout of the fort. Of the 3,000 men in the Regiment, only a platoon of infantrymen could be made available, as the Grenadiers were fighting to retake the two Albert Canal bridges that had been captured intact by the other *Sturmgruppen*. Later in the day, as pressure mounted to hold the line of the Canal, the issue of 7th Infantry Division providing a counter-attack force was out of the question. The failure to provide the fort with a contingent of infantry, or to place infantry under Major Jottrand's command, was a stark omission.

By mid-morning, the Belgian Grenadiers, along with the handful of gunners, were beginning to make their presence felt on the Upper Surface of the fort. *Leutnant* Witzig recalled:

> Some hand-to-hand fighting took place on the western boundary. I sent a strong patrol with reconnaissance orders; we had sent them in the direction of the entry building. I wanted to know what was happening in that direction, whether we had to expect any counter attacks, and if so, what kind; for I could not expect our still-strong opponent who occupied the fort, locked below us, to accept the destruction of his defensive works without mounting counter-attacks. These attempts at reconnaissance caused us too many losses. I couldn't repeat them. But we now knew that the shrubbery on the north western corner of the fort was occupied by enemy lookouts and patrols who were attacking us.

If the *fallschirmjäger* lacked the strength to take on the Grenadiers, the Belgian infantrymen were also reluctant to attack with such a small force, and to brave Witzig's *Spandau* fire

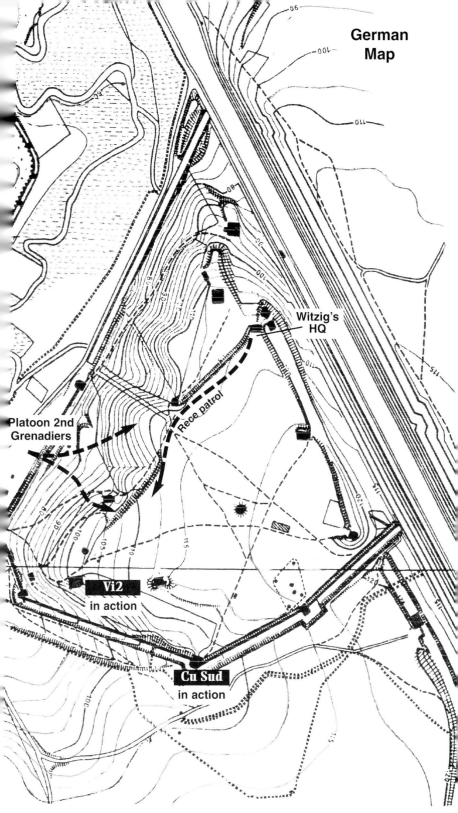

German Map

Witzig's HQ

Rece patrol

Platoon 2nd Grenadiers

Vi2 in action

Cu Sud in action

and bombing by Stukas. Equally, tasking of Belgian artillery fire support for the infantry from either the PFL fortresses or from their own field artillery was so ponderous that it was almost impossible to coordinate a meaningful fire plan to support any attack on the Upper Surface. It is known that a more substantial counter-attack was being organised through Headquarters 7th Infantry Division, but this was cancelled, for reasons that have never been explained.

It is worth noting that there is evidence that the off-duty shift, while marching from Wonk, were tasked by Major Jottrand to mount counter-attacks, and it is reputed that only twelve men eventually made it into the fort 'unwounded and capable'. Hence, the gun crews that were still operational in the casemates did not receive the expected relief, and remained at their positions throughout the battle. However, a few Belgian soldiers remained active in the wooded western edge of the fort for most of the day and *Sous Lieutenant* Verstraeten was amongst those wounded during the fighting on the western edge of the fort.

Cupola 120 (24)   Heiner Lange had earlier detonated a hollow charge on top of the massive steel cupola, which had driven Sergeant Cremer and his men to the Intermediate Level, but after a pep talk, they had returned and continued to try to fix the ammunition-loading mechanism. Meanwhile, the Belgians continued to shoot through the sight housing with a rifle, and traverse the turret to report on German activity on the Upper Surface.

Grechza, one of Haug's men from Section 5, had filled his water bottle with rum and was consequently roaring drunk. He threatened the Belgian prisoners, but was seen off by Heiner Lange. Grechza now turned his attention to the rotating Cupola 120, which he climbed up, and sat astride one of the elevated guns, riding it like a bronco. A furious *Feldwebel* Wenzel saw what was happening. Pointing his pistol at Grechza, he ordered Grechza off the cupola and then threw pre-prepared 2.5 kilo charges into both gun barrels. Inside the cupola, the detonations shook the gun crews, with some gunners being thrown down the ladders to the level below. Flames from the explosion seared the crew. Again, Sergeant Cremer herded all below and hastily erected the barrier of steel beams and sand bags between the

140

One of the 120 mm barrels damaged by 2.5 kilo charges.

Right: The steps down which the gunners were blown by the exploding charges.

two steel doors.

Eventually electricity to Cupola 120 was restored, the fumes and dust raised by the explosions could be extracted, and the Cupola reoccupied on the orders of the Battery Commander.

Rene Cremer was quickly occupying his seat and peering through the gun site:

I immediately inspected the surrounding terrain and saw parachutes descending slowly, supporting a kind of shell of great size [a stores container]. *A German rushes up to it as soon as it lands, and extracts from it ammunition and stores. Seeing all these weapons of destruction, I think that one of them is perhaps destined for me, and that it will serve to send us into the hereafter...*

Staying at the lookout, I was able to make out the system of

141

signalling used by the enemy parachutists on the hill. To show the place where the planes should drop their parachutes, the Germans put big panels on the ground with swastikas on them. I was able to make one of them bite the dust with the help of my rifle, fired as usual through the telescope emplacement.

Wanting to find out what repairs were necessary to the cupola, I put Van Gelooven, Malchair and Gysens on the cupola's firing level, and ordered them to watch very carefully and fire rifles at anyone who approached.

'After inspecting the guns, I realised that the left weapon was unusable; the breech was destroyed. So I informed the Command Post and promised Lieutenant Dehousse to do all I can to repair the right gun, but work only advanced very slowly. To avoid more unpleasant surprises, I incessantly rotate the cupola... For too many hours, we struggled with this unlucky gun, but it was

The massive breech of one of the 120 mm guns that Cremer and his men repaired.

An external view of the same gun.

with great satisfaction that I could announce to my firing officer that the repair was finished. The Lieutenant who has come back embraced everybody and returned to his office.

As he left, I had begged him to give me an order to fire as quickly as possible; it was a long wait, in spite of 4 or 5 telephone calls. I wanted to take the initiative and load the gun, but without any precise target and without news from outside, I was forced to give up my desire to open fire.

While waiting, Cremer had other things to think about; like many of the other senior NCOs at the fort, his family were at home at Lanaye.

I ask myself a whole set of questions. What's going on at Lanaye? Is it occupied by the enemy? Was it bombarded? Have... my family been evacuated? A thousand thoughts come to mind and I have to make a big effort to control them.

Cremer continued his account:

Still no order to fire and I decide to unload the gun. The shell was barely extracted when bullets whistled through the barrel into the cupola. I jump on the closing system and the breech is barely sealed when a violent explosion throws me to the ground. I got up and made the men go down. Several explosions followed one after another, causing damage, and immense flames took over the whole cupola. The air was unbreathable, and with my eyes streaming I leaned against the security door. This building,

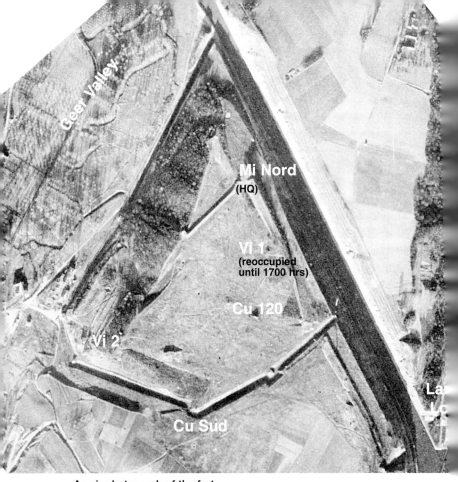

Geer Valley

Mi Nord
(HQ)

Vi 1
(reoccupied
until 1700 hrs)

Cu 120

Vi 2

Cu Sud

An air photograph of the fort.

for which I owed my existence in the army, and to which the whole crew was attached, had just been reduced to silence by some Teutonic bandits. Getting over my misery, I pushed myself to re assemble my men; luckily none was wounded or burned.

I had the crew put on their gas masks, and eventually we reoccupied the cupola, but alas, the guns were completely unusable and only the Royal Foundry's cannon team could have repaired them. Our only task now was to watch the hill, and we took it in turns to be the spotter.

I had been at the observation post for nearly half an hour. I still had not seen anything until I suddenly saw a Boche standing up about five metres from my cupola. Taking aim at him and in spite of only being able to see his stomach, I pulled *the trigger. The shot flew out; the "grey" grabbed at his stomach, shouted two or three times and then fell never to rise again.*

From time to time, we were violently shaken by the shock wave, violent explosions occurring in the immediate area of the building [probably bombs dropped by Stukas]... *Our only consolation was to hear our comrades of Cupola S and Vi 2 firing frequently.*

A little later, the aiming telescope was suddenly obscured. As I shouted to warn my men to take cover, I was violently thrown over. I heard someone shout "I'm wounded!" It was my brave comrade Van Gelooven who had been struck down by the explosion. I helped him down in an almost unbreathable atmosphere and I was wounded myself.

Cupola Sud (23) The report made at the behest of the Germans by the Belgian crew in the prisoner-of-war camp reads:

Despite the dive bombing by the Stukas, with their screaming sirens, which at any moment might destroy the cupola, the intermittent noise of the Germans attacking the nearby Bloc V, the fire of Fort of Pontisse, and the scraps of news received in morsels that most of the defence works had exploded or been put out of action, the crew of Cupola Sud continued to accomplish their missions. Tribute must be paid to them, for their tenacity with which they maintained barrage firing at the defences on the Meuse and the Albert Canal, as well as firing directly on the enemy already in the Geer valley [Objective Eisen] *and also on the high ground at the Loverix Mill, which was the German rendezvous.*

This firing of conventional high explosive shells was interspersed with engagements with canister rounds, designed to prevent the enemy from approaching the cupola and attacking them from the cover of the other casemates. 'This courageous battle lasted till around 1100 hours on the 11 of May: at this moment, virtually alone among all the defensive works of the fort, Cupola Sud still held out.' The German analysis, that a position that was not neutralised in the first wave of attacks would be difficult if not impossible to subdue, was clearly correct.

Visé 1 (26) By 0800 hours the gap between the two doors at the foot of the stairwell had been filled with barriers of small steel I-

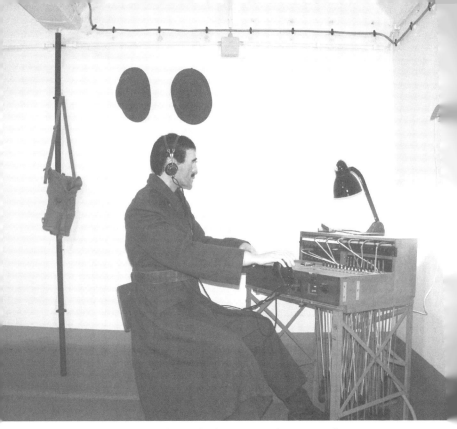

The telephone exchange in the command post complex.

beams, and an additional barricade of sand bags was built in the 'Gallery of Triangles'. A little later, at about 1000 hours:

> Commandant *Van der Auwera ordered* Leutnant *Desloover, Mdlis Delcourt and two men to retake Vi 1; they went up* [to the casemate] *again after having removed the barrier of beams. The casemate is found not to be occupied by the Germans and the two guns that are found to be usable are brought into action.*

However, at 1030 hours, again on the orders of Command Post, Visé 1 ceased fire in order to allow the platoon from 2nd Grenadiers to counter-attack. It is recorded that 'The crew again withdrew down from the casemate to the Intermediate Level'.

At 1200 hours, the Belgian telephone logs show that reports were issued to Headquarters PFL that the casemate had been lost. In this situation, it is probable that the gun crews had gone down to the Intermediate Level for safety and had not answered the phone. Consequently, with most of the other casemates

146

having been knocked out and the phones on occasions being answered by Germans, the Command Post drew what was to them an obvious conclusion. Despite erroneous reports, Visé 1's gun crews, with their shaky morale, remained in action, intermittently, until 1700 hours. At this hour, the *fallschirmjäger* dropped 1 kilo explosive charges into each barrel.

'The violent explosions and smoke produced the final evacuation of the casemate, and a barrier of steel I-beams was finally set in place at the foot of the well. The crews of Visé 1 manned the barricades that they had earlier built in the 'Gallery of Triangles'.

Penetrating the Fort

With most of the fort's offensive elements neutralised or at least working at a greatly reduced capacity, *Leutnant* Witzig explained that it was not enough to have neutralised the offensive casemates:

What we had to do was, on the one hand, to shake the enemy deep under our positions as much as possible by heavy explosions, and on the other hand, to prevent him from coming up to us in the casemates which we had taken, but were occupying with so few men.

A really important action on our part was detonating charges in the depths below various buildings. The casemates that we had penetrated generally had a staircase and a lift, by which we could reach the fort's lower levels.

Maastricht 1 (12)

Feldwebel Arent, commanding Section 3, recalled that:

It was necessary for us to re-enter the casemate to escape the action of the Stukas who were bombing within 200 metres of us. The attack of the Stukas reinforced our morale, as the enemy started bombarding the exterior of the massif with artillery fire, but we suffered very badly [in the casemate] *from the lingering smoke of our explosions.*

Having sheltered from the Belgian artillery fire and the blast from their own Stuka's bombs along with his prisoners, Arent discovered that there was no sound of activity on the level below:

I decided to go into the interior of the fort, but before going down, I ensured that the hole we had made to get in was secure

One of the double doors at the foot of the stairway up to Ma 1. One layer of steel beams are in place and the void partly filled by sandbags.

from counter-attack from the outside. M and H followed me down to the lower level, which we inspected. There was nothing but ammunition and a lavatory. We went down about 118 steps, but we had to jump a number of holes that the Belgians had opened on the landings.'

The staircase wound down from the casemate's lower chamber around the ammunition hoist, but the retreating Belgians had lifted the plates on three of the landings – the ones that could be removed to facilitate the raising and lowering of heavy equipment. This slowed Arent's descent down the stairwell to the fort's Intermediate Level. Having reached the bottom of the flight of stairs, he found the twin doors from the chamber shut and barricaded against him with steel girders and sandbags. He could go no further, and returned back up to the casemate.

Late that evening, *Feldwebel* Arent retraced his steps down the staircase from Ma 1 to the still-silent chamber on the Intermediate Level. This time he and one of his men were each carrying a section of a 50 kilo hollow charge, with which he intended to attack the airlock doors that gave access to the galleries and the heart of the fort.

Arent lit the extended fuse that he had rigged up, and dashed back up the stairs. The resulting explosion in the confined space destroyed the stairway and the ammunition hoist. The hollow charge tore through the steel door and beams, and, making short work of the sandbags, blew metal fragments and one of the doors into the gallery beyond. The explosion's blast travelled down the narrow galleries and destroyed the barricade that had been built near Vi 1, and bowled men over, breaking bones and concussing others. Fragments punctured barrels of weak chlorine-based cleaning fluid that were stacked in the corridor and the resulting odour of chlorine was

The effect of the explosion on the ammunition hoist and stairway can still be examined sixty-five years later.

Ma I's door was blown off its mounting by the charge detonated by *Feldwebel* Arent.

circulated around the fort by the ventilation system, causing the Belgians to put on their gas masks. While what was initially thought to be a gas attack did not cause panic, it did serve to add uncertainty, and further undermined the morale of most of those not confined in the Intermediate and Lower Levels. Many of the garrison reported painful headaches which have been attributed to the chlorine.

In accordance with Witzig's strategy of maintaining pressure on the Belgians by taking the battle to them, other hollow charges were carried down to the Intermediate Level from both Mi Nord and Mi Sud during the course of the night of 10/11 May.

Visé 2   While the forts of the PFL and the Belgian field artillery principally engaged the central and southern part of the fort, and a few hardy individuals sniped at the Germans from the scrub on the western flank, Henri Lecluse was still present in

The doorway int the chamber be Ma 1 clearly showing the damage caused the blast of a 50 kilo hollow char The *fallschirmjä* took the battle t the Belgian defenders, blasti their way into the heart of the fortress.

one of the casemates that had not been subdued by the *fallschirmjäger*. He wrote that the crew lost track of time, but Lecluse clearly remembers being given the first information to supplement the briefest of situation reports received over the telephone from the Battery Command Post:

> *Lieutenant Delcourt alerted us to the possibility that our casemate may be blown up in the same way as Ma 1 and 2 had been. This did not improve our confidence! We were told that there were dead and wounded, and from this moment, we were pursued by the thought of a similar fate.*

Tiredness and hunger were another common theme in accounts. Lecluse reported:

> *During the period between firing engagements, we retired to the rest room, except for the telephonist. If it had not been for our stomachs, nothing would have indicated that it was breakfast time. Two soldiers were delegated to go down to the kitchen, and at the same time, everyone asked the pair to go via the barracks to bring up the food we had stored in our suitcases. After a half hour, they brought us back a cafétiere of coffee, bread and sugar. Everybody fell upon these, and we harassed the men who came back for news – Ma 1 & 2 had been knocked out, along with Cu Nord. They had seen wounded and they had been told about terrible burns to the face of several men. They had been told that the relief crews from Wonk would replace us soon, and we talked of counter-attacks the men from Wonk would make, to rid the top of the fort of parachutists. We were assured by the two men that there were only about a hundred Germans on the upper surface.*

Later in the morning Henri Lecluse recalled that:

> *The CP asked us if we could hear the sound of digging. It seemed to us that we could hear the sound of a rolling stone and as soon as this was alerted to the CP, they ordered Cu Sud to fire on our casemate and Bloc V, which could also machine-gun our walls. For our part, we fired a canister [a shot-gun type] round at elevation 0, which exploded as it left the barrel.*
>
> *In the meantime, to avoid the enemy penetrating into the fort by Ma 2, other soldiers established barricades of sand bags in the tunnels, from behind which, they could fire with the machine guns and rifles that were positioned there. From our position, we could see one of the barricades. To avoid accident we agreed that we would announce ourselves in Walloon. We were equipped with grenades and we loaded our carbines.*

The casemate is supplied with shells for protection firing, but alas, the lift only worked manually – the electrics had never worked properly. At the beginning of the afternoon, a soldier had his finger cut off by accident in the cage. Around 1400 hours some men went down to the kitchen and brought back potatoes and beans.

From time to time I visited the casemate and looked through the sight, and could see the sun, and the football field was full of shell holes and an electrical cable was hanging useless nearby, but I wanted so much to see one of our shells exploding.

Visé 2 remained in action throughout the day, effectively engaging targets to the south of the fort and in support of the other PFL forts, but this was only a small proportion of the fire that the fort was supposed to have delivered. As far as the Germans were concerned fire from the fort against their bridgeheads over the Albert canal was negligible.

Outside, on the Upper Surface of the fort, the *fallschirmjäger* who should have been relieved in the morning were also suffering. *Leutenant* Witzig wrote:

After the hard fighting during the day, the detachment lay, exhausted and parched, under scattered fire from Belgian artillery and infantry outside the fortification; every burst of machine gun fire might have signalled the beginning of the counter-attack we expected, and our nerves were tense.

As darkness fell, Witzig and his men expected to see the *Wehrmacht* pioneers. The volume of firing around Kanne to the immediate north of the fort grew, but no one came. It was going to be a long night for the Germans.

Fallschirmjäger in action operating an MG 34 'Spandau'.

Chapter 8

THE ADVANCE TO THE BRIDGES

General von Reichenau's German Sixth *Armee* considered the route across the River Meuse at Maastricht and the Albert Canal to the north of Eben Emael to be the 'Maastricht Gateway' into Belgium. The fall of Eben Emael was von Reichenau's prerequisite for bringing his considerable concentration of force into action, as this was the sector where he would pierce the Belgian line and then roll up the enemy with his *Blitzkrieg's* 'expanding torrent'. The longer it took to cross the Albert Canal, the greater would be the loss of the advantages of surprise, shock and momentum.

General von Reichenau.

Hitler had feared that unless Eben Emael and the bridges were captured promptly, his panzer spearheads would be halted while his infantry divisions would be drawn into costly and time-consuming engagements to overcome the Albert Canal defences. The Eben Emael area was the 'cork in the bottle' that could ruin the German strategy for overrunning Belgium by allowing time for the Allies to occupy and develop positions in the centre of the country.

Sixth *Armee's* initial attack was to be mounted between Venlo and Aachen by a leading operational echelon of four German Corps consisting of ten infantry divisions. XXVII *Korps* (299th and 263rd Divisions) would attack the Dutch border fortifications east of Maastricht. However, an independent advance guard under direct command of Sixth *Armee*, consisting of the reinforced 4th Panzer Division, was to press on ahead and drive across the Meuse Bridges in the centre of Maastricht. These bridges were to be captured by a detachment from Battalion *zur Besonderen Verwendung* 100 (vbv 100), enabling the advance guard to reach *Sturmabteilung* Koch's bridgeheads on the Albert Canal within six hours. With serious water obstacles in its path, 4th Panzer had significant engineer-

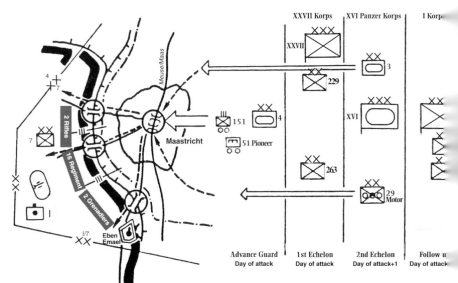

General von Richthofen.

mobility assets under command, mainly in the form of rubber boats and bridging. The second operational echelon, consisting of I and XVI *Korps*, was to be deployed late on Day One and on Two, and was to lead the breakout into the heart of Belgium. 3rd Panzer and 29th Motorised (Panzer Grenadier) Divisions of XVI *Korps* would lead, supported by the slower moving infantry of I *Korps* (11th and 61st Divisions). This considerable force would be supported by a reserve of a further five fresh infantry divisions.

Sixth *Armee* was supported by *Luftwaffe's* VIII *Flieger Korps* commanded by General von Richthofen and 2nd Air Defence Corps commanded by General Desloch. The allocated *Luftwaffe* squadrons were closely integrated in order to provide offensive air support, with *Stuka* aircraft, and air defence by anti-aircraft guns or combat air patrols.

The balance of ground forces about to be committed to battle in the Maastricht Gateway less Eben Emael was:

Category	Belgian	German
Men	15,000	140,000
Tanks	12 Tank destroyers	600, all types
Anti-tank	24 x 47 mm	375, all types
Artillery	40	1,200

Railway
Bridge

151 IR

The Maas/Meuse river in Maastricht, photographed in May 1940 by the RAF,
showing three bridges intact.

N

The southern tongue of Holland, including the city of Maastricht, due to its military isolation, was not strongly held by the Dutch Army.

The Meuse Bridges

The three bridges in the centre of Maastricht were essential for the German plans. Unlike other key points to be attacked by the Germans, they were not as well defended as elsewhere on the front. However, even a lightly defended bridge can be blown by the simple act of pressing a button on a demolition circuit. The attackers therefore needed to take special measures to ensure that this did not happen, as the relatively slow and very noisy panzers approached the river.

The two Meuse Bridges were an obvious objective for a large detachment of vbv 100. A senior staff officer recalled that,

> *4th Panzer Division was to cross the border and advance west on three routes to relieve the* fallschirmjäger *at the bridges, but to do this they had to cross the two bridges in Maastricht. These were to be taken by advance groups from vbv Battalion 100 disguised as Dutch policemen. In advance of the attack, they had infiltrated across the border and had ridden on bicycles to the bridges.*

The reality was more complicated, as the plan had two elements. When the date for the attack on the west had been set, vbv 100 soldiers infiltrated across the border in civilian clothes on 8/9 May and cycled to Maastricht, where they joined others

A 'Fifth Columnist' with his *fallschirmjäger* comrades. His job was to prevent bridges being demolished by the Belgians.

already in position. Their task was to disable the demolition circuits on the bridges without the Dutch being aware of this. This is easier said than done in advance of an attack, however, as military engineers routinely check and test their circuits. Even though the Germans claimed that the Brandenburgers had succeeded in cutting the demolition cables, the circuits were demonstrably working again on 10 May 1940.

The second and larger group or *Sonderverband* (special unit) was under the command of *Hauptmann* Hocke. Thirteen miles to the northeast of Maastricht, near Sittrad, they had crossed the border carefully on bicycles and a few motorcycles at 0320 hours on 10 May. Moving in small groups on different routes, dressed as Dutch Military Police, their task was to bluff their way onto the bridges at dawn, where they were also tasked to disable the demolitions, if this had not been completed by the advance group. However, German invasion plans had been compromised at the last moment by an error in the *Reichsverteidgung* Ministry in Berlin, and the Dutch defenders were at full alert shortly after midnight. Consequently, the fake Military Police were identified before the various groups could get within a mile of the bridges.

The Albert Canal Bridges

From a point just south of Eben Emael, 7th Belgian Infantry Division held well-developed positions north along the Albert Canal. The numerous bridges were all prepared for demolition and each guarded by about a company of infantry from one of the Division's three infantry regiments: the three bridges directly west of Maastricht were the objectives of *Sturmgruppe* Koch. See map on page 22

Where the spoil bank and the canal cutting ran through the surrounding hills, the Albert Canal was in effect in a trench, with high-level bridges. The canal had been developed into a defensive barrier system, and unless these bridges were captured intact, the Germans would find crossing it extremely difficult. Hence the importance of the area to Hitler in his initial plan, and subsequently in the version put into action in May 1940: while the main effort in the Ardennes developed, Sixth *Armee* had to advance into mid Belgium and fix the Franco-British forces in place.

**The view across the widened barge basin to the Kanne Bridge. Note the
high ground that was used by the Belgian grenadiers to good effect.**

Sturm Abteilung Koch

Hauptmann Koch's main effort was to capture the three bridges
across the Albert Canal that ran parallel to the Dutch-Belgian
border. Fort Eben Emael, though very important in its own
right, was the secondary objective, as without the bridges being
captured intact, the momentum of the German advance would
break down while they were captured under the fire of the fort.
Because of the canal's proximity to the border, there was no
Belgian covering force to withdraw, so the Belgians had no
reason to delay blowing the bridges: thus it was considered that
the Panzers would be extremely unlikely to take the bridges
intact by an armoured *coup de main*. But a glider *coup de main*
could deliver the troops to take the bridges in a concentrated
group, with surprise and a coherence that could not be achieved
by parachute.

The 420 *fallschirmjäger* and 42 glider pilots of *Sturmabteilung*
Koch were divided into five groups, four of approximately 80
and one of 100. One group, based on the Divisional Pioneer
Kompanie under *Leutnant* Witzig, was to take the fort, while
three other groups of infantry, also flown in by gliders, were to
seize three of the Albert Canal bridges. The fifth group was
Koch's support weapons group. They were to be dropped by
parachute, some forty minutes after the initial landing, into the
bridgeheads that the assault groups had seized in order to help
the *fallschirmjäger* hold their gains until the arrival of 4th Panzer

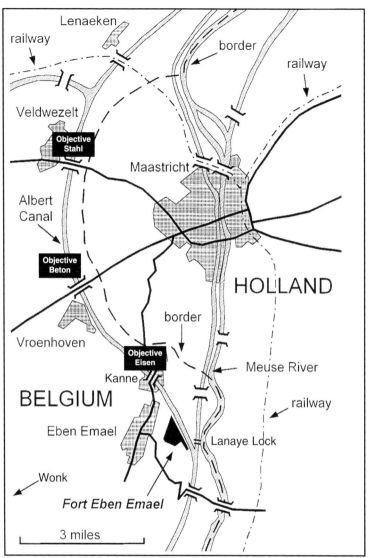

Division. The parachute sorties would be followed five minutes later by supply drops from Heinkel 111 bombers. After the Ju 52 tug aircraft had cast off their DFS 230, they would fly a circuit for fifteen minutes, and then follow the gliders west and drop their on-board cargo of dummy paratroopers to the west of the Albert Canal in the rear of 7th Belgian Infantry Division. Koch himself was to land by glider with the assault troops tasked to capture the bridge at Vroenhoven, Objective *Beton* (Concrete).

The operation started, along with *Leutnant* Witzig's

sturmgruppe at the airfields around Köln: the *coup de main* parties would share the same twelve-minute glide down to their objectives from their cast-off point near Aachen. H-Hour was also to be at 0430 hours Belgian time on 10 May 1940 and the *fallschirmjäger* were briefed to expect relief by 1000 hours the same day; but like most subsequent airborne operations in the next five years of war, this estimate would prove to be optimistic.

Vroenhoven Bridge – Objective *Beton* (Concrete)

As the three *sturmgruppe* headed for the Albert Canal bridges, flying over the southern outskirts of Maastricht at about 2,000 feet, they were met with fire from anti-aircraft machine guns and artillery. This fire and with the aircraft silhouetted against the dawn sky, alerted the Belgians that an attack of some kind was actually imminent.

On the ground, the Vroenhoven Bridge, the centre bridge of the three that *Hauptmann* Koch and his men were to capture, was held by 6th Company of 18 Infantry Regiment. Their concrete bunkers and field defences had been manned for some hours, but with the noise of gunfire, they were alert and standing-to in their defensive positions.

At 0415 hours, ten of the eleven gliders of *Sturmgruppe Beton*, commanded by *Leutnant* Schacht, swept down to land on the western side of the canal. At 300 feet over the bridge, the gliders came under heavy fire from the trenches around the bridge. *Obergefreiter* Stolzewski's glider carrying Section 8 was hit by anti-aircraft fire; the control cables were cut and the glider crashed from about thirty feet. Three soldiers were wounded and were unable to take part in the action. However, most of the gliders landed in their planned locations, less *Oberfeldwebel* Hofmann's DFS 230 that landed 150 yards to the northwest of the vital command-post casemate that he was to attack. Losing another three men wounded, with his *Spandau* damaged and under enemy fire, his surviving five *fallschirmjäger* left the glider and cleared a trench leading to the casemate. As one of his men, *Gefreiter* Stenzel, arrived at the bunker, he saw through the open door that the Belgians were preparing to blow the bridge; at the last moment, he scrambled to cut the demolition cables where they left the casemate and the charges failed.

The gliders that landed near the bridge carried out their

orders as planned, overcoming the surprised defenders with the speed and violence of their attack. *Fallschirmjäger* Röhrich and Giese destroyed the two bunkers at the canal, and the attached pioneers blew up the houses next to the bridge to clear fields of fire.

The infantrymen of *Sturmabteilung* Koch were as well trained and prepared for their specific part in the operation as Witzig's pioneers.

A crucial part of the German plan was an attack by four Stukas on an identified Belgian Headquarters at Lanaken, to coincide with the glider landings. The Belgian report clearly identifies the fact that the authorised demolition commander, *Commandant* Giddeloo, was killed in the attack, along with his staff and radio operators, as they attempted to authorise the

The high level VroenBridge across the deep trench of the Albert Canal is guarded by a large bunker. *Inset:* **the bunker today carrying the N79.**

blowing of the demolitions. It is believed that the Belgian command had failed to delegate authority to blow the bridge to a sufficiently low level for timely action to be taken by the demolition commander, when faced with attack. The Belgians believed that they would have ample warning of an overland approach across Dutch territory, or time to issue orders while paratroopers assembled on their DZs. As with Fort Eben Emael, they had not anticipated the immediate effect of a glider attack. At 0430 hours, *Sturmgruppe Beton* was signalling by radio 'Objective taken'.

It was a very tight bridgehead that had been established around the Vroenhoven Bridge, with only a hundred men facing a regiment (equivalent of a brigade) numbering some 3,000 men. However, while clearing the trenches in the area of the bridge, the Germans claim to have taken three hundred prisoners, who were used to clear the tank obstacles on the road and bridge.

Meanwhile, German pioneers were detailed to remove the explosive charges, cables on the bridge and the demolition chambers in the approach road and abutments. Within half an hour of landing, the bridge was secure. Clearance patrols under *Obergefreiter* Borchardt scoured the area around the bridge out to six hundred yards, while east of the bridge an enemy counter-attack force, thought to be Dutch, came into action. After short but heavy fighting, they were pinned down by *Spandau* fire and the Dutch commander ordered his troops to stop firing and surrendered. Other Dutch soldiers withdrew towards Maastricht.

Hauptmann Koch and *Leutnant* Schacht established their headquarters by the bridge's abutments under cover of the roadway. The Belgians who had lost the bridge did not withdraw but poured fire into the German bridgehead from the hills to the west and only at 1032 hours were the *fallschirmjäger* able to signal that bridgeheads had been properly secured.

Forty minutes after the landing, the support-weapons group jumped from Ju 52s in the area east of the bridge, landing astride the road. One man landed in the canal and drowned, another was hit in the air and killed. The machine guns they brought made a welcome reinforcement and helped to see off enemy counter-attacks along with air support by Stukas. Supply drops followed as planned.

The dropping of dummy parachutists added confusion, and already scant Belgian reserves were directed away from the bridges and fort, so *Leutnant* Schacht had the opportunity to consolidate his positions before the Belgians of 18 Infantry Regiment could mount serious counter-attacks from the west. Later, as the pressure from 18 Infantry Regiment's counter-attacks increased, the *fallschirmjäger* counted the hours until their relief arrived; but with the Meuse Bridges blown, the news was not good.

The Veldwezelt Bridge – Objective *Stahl* (Steel)

At the northern Albert Canal bridge of the three, the demolition guard was provided by *2nd Rifle Regiment*, whose three battalions were deployed on a frontage of four and a half miles, up to the divisional boundary with 4th Infantry Division. They were to face *Oberleutnant* Gustav Altmann and the ninety-two men of *Sturmgruppe Stahl*.

As the nine gliders came into land at 0424 (0524) hours, the Belgian *Rifles* did not hesitate, and opened fire on the fragile DFS 230 gliders as they made their final approach. The leading pilot, *Unteroffizier* Stuhr, crouching in his cockpit, was struck in the head. With his hands off the aircraft's controls and with a section of his wing shot away, he crash-landed from an altitude of about thirty feet, injuring all but two of the men aboard. This

Veldwezelt Bridge. Note the machine gun embrasures in the pillars that cover the canal.

left just seventy *fallschirmjäger, plus pilots,* to capture the objective, but the landing of the rest of the group was scattered, due largely to a patch of spring fog in the valley. The glider with Section 6 aboard landed 1000 yards from the objective, while another landed around 400 yards from the bridge. Section 2's glider turned over during a crash landing but only one soldier was seriously injured, with a broken arm. But the surprise of the glider attack was a clear force multiplier: even though the Belgians were fully alert, *Sturmgruppe Stahl* successfully assaulted the Belgian *Rifles's* positions, fighting through trenches towards the concrete pillbox that overlooked the bridge. The *fallschirmjäger* saw that the pillbox's door was open, so they threw in hand grenades and three 2kgs explosive charges. The section then blew up a building next to the bridge with two pre-prepared box charges along with three other Belgian houses, again to clear fields of fire.

Another major machine gun bunker was built into the western abutment of the bridge, which was knocked out by the Pioneer Section whose grenades killed or wounded its fifteen-man garrison. Meanwhile, with their enemy in the immediate area of the bridge neutralised, the pioneers set about clearing the bridge of detonating circuits and explosives, all the while under heavy enemy fire. Even though one of the pillboxes was still holding out, *Oberleutnant* Altmann reported over the radio at 0435 hours that the `Veldwezelt objective is taken'.

Oberleutnant Altmann commander of Sturmgruppe Stahl.

In broad daylight, squadrons of roving Stuka dive-bombers supported the *fallschirmjäger* for about an hour before being tasked to support the Sixth *Armee* advance elsewhere. Swastika air-identification panels marking the German bridgeheads helped the airmen to identify German held positions, and with their distinctive sirens wailing, dive into attacks on Belgian troop concentrations before they could counter-attack the bridgeheads. While the Belgians were under attack from the air, with reports that parachutists were being dropped behind them, and with Eben Emael, the world's most powerful fortress, itself under attack and only able to provide limited fire support, it is not surprising that the Belgians were temporarily neutralised.

At 0515 hours, the *fallschirmjägers'* support group was

Wehrmacht infantry re-enact the taking the surrender of the Belgian defenders.

parachuted in to reinforce the bridgehead. Again, the drop was dispersed, with the aircraft coming in under heavy machine gun fire. One *Spandau* crew landed about 1000 yards to the west, where one of the *fallschirmjäger* was killed, another was lightly wounded, and the parachute of one of the machine gunners failed to open. Those that landed in one piece, having opened the two weapon containers under enemy fire, promptly cleared

Fallschirmjäger along with supply containers being dropped from a Ju 52.

the *Rifles* from a trench alongside their drop zone. The machine gun crew that landed to the west was isolated, but took up a position from which they engaged the enemy with flanking fire.

From about 0530 hours, the enemy organised several counter-attacks on the Veldwezelt Bridgehead, which were repelled by the *fallschirmjäger's* disciplined fire. An ensuing lull ended at 0800 hours, when the first really strong and organised Belgian counter-attack was mounted from the northwest. It was beaten off by a combination of close air support by the *Luftwaffe* and small-arms fire, and then fresh Stukas prevented the Belgians from reorganising and resuming the attack.

There followed another pause in the battle, during which several Belgian machine guns southwest of the bridge kept the *fallschirmjäger* under fire from a range of about 500 yards. At 0900 hours, Belgian artillery and mortar fire began but slackened after the Stukas responded to a call for close air support. At about this time, *Sturmgruppe Stahl* established radio contact with a flak battalion by radio and 'the requested and corrected 88 mm gun fire which was very effective' [against ground targets].

After the Stukas had withdrawn again, four Belgian light T 13 tanks from the slim armoured resources available to 7th Infantry Division probed towards the Veldwezelt Bridge. But fire from German anti-tank rifles knocked out two of the T 13s, and the remaining tanks withdrew, along with their supporting infantry.

Around midday, Belgian artillery and mortars again engaged the *fallschirmjäger* but were promptly neutralised by an air attack. The Germans at the bridge received a considerable boost when, shortly before 1300 hours, an artillery observer party arrived at the bridge from the Maastricht crossings. Taking a position overlooking the bridge, the *Wehrmacht* gunners were able to bring effective artillery fire on the road to Hasselt. The first German infantry elements, a platoon of the 3rd Battalion, 151 Infantry, and a support section, arrived at 1330 hours and reinforced the bridgehead.

In the early evening, the Belgians engaged the bridge with artillery fire, but the German *Schtzen Regiment 33* were now arriving and taking over and expanding the bridgehead. The opportunity to retake the vital crossing and restore the defensive line had passed.

At 2130 hours *Sturmabteilung* Koch had been withdrawn from

Fallschirmjäger with collected parachute.

the Veldwezelt and Vroenhoven Bridges and marched back towards Maastricht. *Sturmgruppe Stahl* suffered casualties totalling 8 dead, 14 severely wounded and 16 light wounded. Belgian casualties were about 85 dead and 200 prisoners.

The Kanne Bridge – Objective *Eisen* (Iron)

Leutnant Martin Schächter commanded the force that was to capture the bridge at Kanne. As far as Koch was concerned, this was the most immediately important bridge as it was required by 4th Panzer Division's advance guard, elements of 51st Pioneer Battalion and 2nd Battalion, 151 Infantry Regiment, to reach the fort. Once across the Albert Canal they were to join *Sturmgruppe Granit* and complete the capture of the fort. However, during the fly-in, one of *Sturmgruppe Eisen's* gliders became lost in the dark before dawn, leaving just nine for the assault on the bridge at Kanne.

The Belgian defenders were from *2 Regiment de Grenadiers*, who held both the bridge and the area surrounding Fort Eben Emael. In addition, they also had primary responsibility for mounting counter-attacks on the fort. With *Sturmgruppe Eisen* landing somewhat after the other *Sturmgruppen*, it was clear to the defenders that an attack was under way. In addition, the fort's observation post at the bridge had been telephoned with a warning. Consequently, the gliders were under fire as they turned into their landing.

Section 1's glider had released its tow before it had reached the requisite height and, consequently, did not reach the landing site astride the bridge but came down on the high ground of Castert, about a mile south west of the objective. Section 9's glider landed about two hundred yards south of the bridge near the road to Eben Emael. Gliders of Sections 6 and 7 did not land quite as planned at the western end of the bridge. Section 3's DFS 230 was hit at an altitude of about ninety feet and a tracer round probably set fire to the glider, which crash-landed accurately but burnt out. The remaining six (out of eleven) aircraft landed as planned, but there were casualties from ground fire in nearly all the aircraft.

As was the case with the other bridges, the *fallschirmjäger* were immediately into the attack. However, there was a significant difference at Objective *Eissen*; the Belgian demolition commander was under orders from Major Jottrand to blow the bridge. With the Belgians being on full alert, the bridge's demolition charges would have been fully armed (detonators connected to the charges) and, before the Germans could cut the cables, it would only take a word from the guard commander to detonate the charges.

The bridge was indeed blown by Sergeant Pirene of the Belgian Grenadiers, at 0435 hours, as the *fallschirmjäger* of Section 3 approached their objective, thus delaying *Sturmgruppe Granit's* relief. Meanwhile, Section 3 blew up three houses and the entrance to a bunker at the eastern end of the bridge and went on to capture the occupants of two further bunkers.

With the bridges blown; the Belgian grenadiers in the trenches protecting the area were overcome but machine gun positions on the high ground raked the area around the bridge with fire. Section 8 attacked and destroyed the machine guns

One of the Kanne Bridge blockhouses. The blown bridge is in the background.

Fallschirmjäger **were resupplied by parachute drops. NCOs unpack a medical supplies canister.**

with grenades, while Section 3 took further positions in the valley and a trench system on the northern hill. The para drop of the support weapons platoon overshot its DZ (drop zone) and the *fallschirmjäger* landed 500m further to the west than intended. During the approach, the planes had come under heavy fire and fourteen *fallschirmjäger* were killed and eight wounded. One German was captured near the DZ and became first the first German PoW in Belgian hands. He was handed over to the British before being released at Dunkirk.

The immediate Belgian counter-attacks lacked determination to sweep away the small groups of *fallschirmjäger* and were described as being 'weak and disorganised in the first hour'. Around 1030 hours a large Belgian force was seen assembling for a counter-attack but they were beaten off by concentrated small arms fire before they could press home their attack. Later, another twenty-five demoralised Belgians, including an officer surrendered to Section 3 in the village of Kanne and a bunker on the Caster Heights surrendered around mid-day.

Sturmgruppe Eisen's radio operator had set up his radio by the ruined bridge and transmitted the message 'Objective reached, resistance strong, bridge blown up. Still passable with preps by pioneers'. However, this was not picked up by *Hauptmann* Koch at Vroenhoven and as a result, he eventually had to send a patrol to find out what was happening at Kanne. That failure at Kanne to communicate led to *VIII Fliegerkorps'* aircraft bombing the *fallschirmjäger* until they managed, under fire from the surrounding high ground, to lay out swastika air recognition panels.

During subsequent fighting, as the Belgians tried to drive the *fallschirmjäger* away from the bridge, *Leutnant* Schächter was seriously wounded, with command being taken over by *Leutnant* Joachim Meissner.

The Advance of 4th Panzer Division
As reports of success by the *fallschirmjäger* on the Albert Canal were coming into the German Headquarters at 0435 (0535) hours, the *Wehrmacht* crossed the borders in a very well coordinated attack. The two infantry divisions of XVII Corps advanced on foot against limited Dutch resistance, put up by just five battalions of border guards. Designated routes were left open for 4th Panzer Division to dash for the bridges at Maastricht and on across the Albert Canal.

Leading the armoured drive to the Meuse Bridge were the

A panzer seen here just inside Dutch territory.

motorcyclists of 7th Recce Battalion. They were to be followed by 151 Infantry Regiment, which had been detached from 61st Infantry Division to 4th Panzer. They were mounted in trucks in order to keep up with a battalion of tanks from 35 Panzer Regiment with whom they were grouped to spearhead the German drive west. A panzer commander on the southerly of three routes taken by the advance guard recalled:

The battalion of Panzer Regiment 35 at the head of the left marching group crossed over the border to the north of Aachen at 0535 (0435 hours Belgian time) hours without resistance and after about two kilometres they reached the main road from Maastricht and drove along this as far as Gulpen. There, however, they met the enemy, who had blown up the Geul crossings and was positioned behind the ruined bridge with anti-tank guns.

Overcoming this first obstacle belt and associated Dutch defences, took over an hour and a half but as the panzer commander recalled:

We drove down into the Maas valley, at around about 0730 hours (0630 Belgian time) and the Maas [Meuse] Bridge blew up into the air in front of us. At the station on the right-hand bank of the Maas we met a motor cycle section from the zbv Wecke battalion who hadn't arrived in Maastricht any earlier than we had. We then pushed through as far as the bridge position, consolidated there and had a shooting match with the Dutch who were in positions on the other side. After an 88 mm anti-aircraft gun had drawn up and taken a shot at the other side, the Dutch surrendered with a white flag and the way was now set for the engineers to set off across the Maas in rafts.

4th Panzer Division's plan included the attachment of two companies of engineers from 51st Pioneer Battalion to the leading columns. In case of failure by vbv 100 and the *fallschirmjäger*, they had obstacle-crossing equipment prepared for immediate use. Within an hour the first of the rafts capable of taking men and light vehicles across the Meuse was in operation. Consequently, according to a panzer officer,

By about 0900 hours, the pioneers of Battalion 51 went on ahead to Kanne, aboard requisitioned Dutch lorries and on bicycles. Meanwhile, Commander 4th Panzer regrouped his force and allocated crossing priority to two infantry Kampfgruppen of 151 Infantry Regiment, who were to head as

German infantry in rubber boats crossing the Maas at Maastricht.

quickly as possible to the two Albert Canal Bridges that were still standing. One pioneer officer recounted that:

'We had ready made-up temporary bridge sections on our vehicles, which were now off-loaded and fixed between the two halves of the large Maastricht bridges which having been poorly destroyed were hanging down into the river.'

These inadequately blown bridges became sites for improvised foot bridges, while the first rafts capable of carrying heavier 8 and 4 tonne vehicles were operating between 1100 and 1200 hours. Thereafter, vehicles trickled forward to join the infantry of the two *Kampfgruppen* strung out on the roads to Objectives *Stahl* and *Beton*, which were just two and a half miles away. Ferrying was slow and only small and lightweight components of the various units could be carried across the river but once on the enemy bank, they immediately set off for their objectives.

While ferrying operations for personnel, lighter equipment and vehicles was under way, other engineers worked at the

173

A Panzer Mk III Maastricht.

Motorcycle reconnaissance troops spearhead the advance west

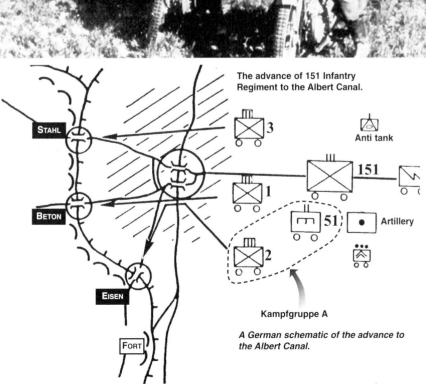

The advance of 151 Infantry Regiment to the Albert Canal.

STAHL

BETON

EISEN

FORT

3

1

2

151

51

Anti tank

Artillery

Kampfgruppe A

A German schematic of the advance to the Albert Canal.

Men of 51 Pioneer Battalion sitting atop a pre inflated rubber assault boat.

Meuse crossings to build ferries and bridges capable of taking 4th Panzer Division's tanks and heavier vehicles. This armour was necessary to consolidate the Albert Canal bridgeheads and act as a springboard for an advance into the centre of Belgium by XVI Corps on Day Two of the offensive. The loss of the Maastricht bridges was a serious setback but the pioneers worked hard to improvise crossings.

The first contact with *Sturmabteilung* Koch was made by 151 Infantry Regiment at Objective *Stahl* at around 1300 (1400) hours and shortly afterwards at the other crossings. However, these leading elements were mainly observation recce and command groups, with very little combat power but as further troops and support weapons arrived, they were fed across the canal into the two bridgeheads. 151 Infantry Regiment did not fully take over *Stahl* and *Beton* until around 2000 hours. German casualties at *Stahl* numbered eight killed and thirty wounded.

Earlier in the afternoon, however, the leading infantry elements had arrived in time to help defeat an attack by a few French light tanks. These vehicles belonging to the 3rd Light Mechanised Division (3 DLM), had dashed about 150 miles in an attempt to reinforce a crucial point in the Belgian lines, in less

175

German infantry attacking a Belgian position 10 May.

than twelve hours, having been unable to enter Belgium until the Germans had violated her neutrality. The tanks had suffered the usual breakdowns and had to brave the harrying *Luftwaffe* air interdiction patrols. Consequently, the detachment arrived with little combat power and were shocked to find that the vital crossings that they were to reinforce were already in German hands. The light French tanks' speculative probes were seen off by the *fallschirmjäger* and 151 Infantry Regiment's light anti-tank weapons.

The heavy pontoons began ferrying the first panzers across the Meuse and the first 16 tonne bridge built across the river at Maastricht, opened at dawn on 11 May. The blowing of the bridges by the Dutch had caused a potentially crucial twenty hour delay to Sixth *Armee* but with two bridgeheads in place over the Albert Canal served by permanent structures capable of bearing the heaviest military equipment, the Maastricht Gateway had been kicked open.

The Bridge at Kanne

The Belgians mounted better-organised counter-attacks on the beleaguered *fallschirmjäger* from the west and southwest at 1500 and 1800 hours but were both repelled with the assistance of artillery fire and close air support. Clearly the integrated communications from *Sturmgruppe Eisen* to *Hauptmann* Koch and supporting arms were working well and the men around the bridge benefited from the work of artillery observers on the high ground to the east, who had been amongst the first elements of 4th Panzer to close up to the canal line during the afternoon.

During the evening, a significant force from Infantry Regiment 2/151 and Pioneer Battalion 51 arrived at the Canal, having been held up by fire from enemy positions in the village of Kanne since the leading elements crossed the Meuse in the early afternoon. With them came over *Leutnant* Witzig's Section 2, who had made their forced landing at Duren before dawn. Section Commander Max Maier was killed in the fighting at Kanne.

A staff officer from 4th Panzer Division summed up the situation:

> *Infantry Regiment 151 and Pioneer Battalion 51 arrived at Kanne in the afternoon. When they reached the town, they immediately came under fire from the Belgians. The* fallschirmjäger *were so weakened by their losses that they were unable to extend their bridgehead so as to push back the Belgians who still held the heights, beyond firing range of the canal. This made a quick crossing impossible and it became apparent that only a properly prepared attack had any chance of success.*

German troops crossing the Maas single file on an improvised footbridge in Maastricht.

Crossing under fire from the Belgians.

Faced with a 'bridgehead', connected by a blown bridge, of little practical military value, the commander of *Kampfgruppe* A, *Oberleutnant* Hans Mikosch, looking down on the canal had to revise his plan. Mikosch's pioneers, supported by infantry of 151 Regiment, had very little equipment with them, due to the blowing of the Meuse bridges and they were confronted with the nightmare scenario, a second waterway with a blown bridge and lightly armed *fallschirmjäger* desperately awaiting relief on the other side. A pioneer officer described *Kampfgruppe* A's hastily made plan for the evening of 10 May:

> *The 2nd* Kompanie *in which I was operations officer, had been ordered to get across remains of the wrecked bridge on to the western bank of the Albert Canal in the dusk twilight to reconnoitre with the* fallschirmjäger *there and to extend the bridgehead. From the protection of the bridgehead, the first and third assault companies would then proceed with full equipment to Fort Eben Emael.*

Several *fallschirmjäger* from Section 8 swam back across the canal during the evening to help lead reinforcements forward. As the attempt to

A German inflatable crosses the Albert Canal

cross the canal got under way, the volume of enemy small-arms and artillery fire started to increase.

While *2nd Kompanie* were attempting to clamber across the blown canal bridge under a withering machine gun fire, *Feldwebel* Portstefen and seventeen pioneers, of *1st Kompanie* attempted to paddle across the river but like their fellows at the bridge they were beaten back. The attempted crossing of the Albert Canal at Kanne and reach *Sturmgruppe Granit* on the evening of 10 May 1940 had failed.

Oberleutnant Witzig, commanding the *Sturmgruppe* in the fort waiting to be relieved, wrote of the pioneers' attempt to reach them:

> *Their attempts to cross in rubber dinghies were made extremely difficult by the shooting from emplacement 17 [Canal Nord], by the side of the canal – we could ourselves hear the gunfire far below us. Eventually we managed to bring this emplacement under partial control by using hanging charges to block the lookout slits in the observation bell with smoke and dirt.*

After a lull in the artillery fire, the Belgians mounted a serious attack on the Kanne bridgehead at about 0030 hours but Infantry Regiment 151 and Pioneer Battalion 51 were now concentrated on the canal and were able to provide copious fire support to the *fallschirmjäger* on the opposite bank.

A German MG 34 team provide covering fire.

Chapter 9

THE SECOND DAY

Reports differ widely as to what happened at Eben Emael overnight on 10/11 May. The Germans needed to maintain some activity to ensure their moral ascendancy over the Belgians and to keep them in their casemates and the lower levels of the fort, but after a largely sleepless night for both sides prior to the attack, the pace of activity must have slackened. Also, despite a generous supply of explosives being flown in with *Sturmgruppe Granit* and the resupply drops early in the morning, the Germans' ammunition was insufficient to mount many raids on the casemates and the interior.

If the Germans were slumbering fitfully with sentries posted waiting for a serious counter-attack, the gun crews fared little better. Henri Lecluse in Visé 2 recalled that 'Sleeping on the concrete floor under greatcoats was cold and drafty, and from time to time we heard the ventilator of Bloc VI and a siren'. He continued:

> *The Command Post won't relieve the casemate. At one point I went down to the barracks and passed the barrier at the star crossroads, where Captain Blanched was white with fear, which was not very encouraging for us. All we can hear is the normal sound of the generator, and nothing seems unusual. The corridors are deserted and there is no sign of the wounded – funny sort of war. In the kitchen, the head chef is burning documents, which did not bode well.*

Kampfgruppe A

Oberleutnant Mikosch, who had been unable to make a significant crossing of the Canal before dark on the evening of 10 May, but had beaten off a Belgian counter-attack on the *fallschirmjäger* holding the Kanne Bridge around midnight, had to think again. This time he was able to base his plan on the full strength of his *Kampfgruppe*, made up of 2 Battalion of Infantry Regiment 151 and and

Oberleutnant Mikosch.

181

two companies of his own Pioneer Battalion 51. He divided them into three groups with a full complement of rubber boats for an assault crossing before dawn at around 0400 hours, Belgian time. Each group consisted of an infantry company and a pioneer company. The pioneers had two roles: some paddled the rubber boats, while others acting as assault pioneers were prepared to attack and overcome fixed fortifications with flamethrowers and explosives. Of course, completing the capture of Fort Eben Emael was the prime objective.

Despite the flames of burning buildings and the occasional flare illuminating the scene, the Germans' first wave of the assault achieved a degree of surprise, and the three assault groups gained a foothold on the far bank. Significantly, *Fallschirmjäger Feldwebel* Harlos's efforts to block Canal Nord's machine-gun and observation positions by lowering explosive charges in to the embrasures, seem to have been at least partly successful, as the quantity of machine-gun fire that *Gruppe Nur 1* [(*5th Kompanie* (Infantry) and *1st Kompanie* (Pioneers)] endured was not nearly as heavy as *Oberfeldwebel* Portsteffen had experienced during his first attempt. Even so, most of the German casualties were incurred during the crossing of the canal.

While the pioneers carried out the assault crossing the infantry gave covering fire.

With concurrent German attacks from the Vroenhoven and Veldwezelt bridgeheads, along with a return of the Stuka dive-bombers, the Belgian response was not as concentrated as before. Consequently, by 0600 hours Mikosch's *Kampfgruppe A* had joined a much relieved *Leutnant* Meissner and his small group of *fallschirmjäger*, and established a viable bridgehead around the Kanne Bridge (Objective *Eisen*), with *Gruppe Nur 2* and 3, while *Gruppe Nur 1* prepared to attack the fort.

Oberfeldwebel Portsteffen and his platoon of pioneers made their way along the wet moat on

Numerous water barriers had to be overcome during the invasion of Holland and Belgium.

Leutnant Meissner.

the northwestern side of the fort, covered by infantry and heavier fire support. The plan was to knock out Bloc II, which alone adequately covered this approach to the fort. Meanwhile, *5th Kompanie* dragged anti-tank guns further south down the

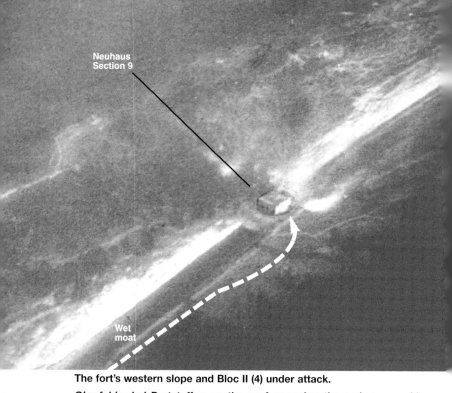

Neuhaus
Section 9

Wet
moat

The fort's western slope and Bloc II (4) under attack.

Oberfeldwebel Portsteffen on the roof engaging the embrasure with a flamethrower.

Geer Valley to engage Blocs I and VI, along with *Spandaus*, which opened fire at about 0700 hours.

The crew of Bloc II had earlier been subjected to attack, with hollow charges being detonated on the observation bell by the *fallschirmjäger*. Now *Oberfeldwebel* Portsteffen was engaging the embrasures with a flamethrower. The Bloc was only silenced, however, when a 50 kilo charge was exploded against one of the embrasures, killing one of the Belgian gunners and wounding six more. The Germans now had a route up onto the surface, and *Oberfeldwebel* Portsteffen climbed up the scrub-covered slop to link up with the *fallschirmjäger* of *Feldwebel* Neuhaus's Section 9. They were shortly joined by an 'elated [and no doubt relieved] *Leutnant* Witzig'. Witzig recalled:

On the 11 of May at about 0700 hours, the first assault troop of the Pioneer Battalion 51, under the leadership of Oberfeldwebel *Portsteffen, came up to us at our post. He succeeded in reaching building 4, which we had repeatedly attacked, but which had been repeatedly re-occupied by the Belgians, by way of the canal cul-de-sac. Of course, we were overjoyed that this link up with the Pioneer Battalion had been achieved. And it was also clear to us that from then on we wouldn't have to deal with a counter-attack from the Belgians.*

Bloc II still showing evidence of heavy fighting.

Rudolf Witzig.

Witzig and Portsteffen formulated a joint plan to break into the fort. This involved blowing as many of the surviving casemates as possible, and gaining control of the area around the fort's entrance. Dropping charges down the gun barrels was a favoured method.

Further anti-tank guns and infantry moved around to the south of the fort, all but enveloping it. Bloc VI reported opening fire at 0820 hours. Its target was 7 *Kompanie* and elements of 3 Pioneer *Kompanie* from the Kanne Bridge.

Events Inside the Fort

After an uneasy night, Major Jottrand had been made aware of the Germans' successful crossing by his observers in Bloc Canal Nord, and had received further depressing news on the situation from HQ PFL and 7th Division. However, determined to fight on, he sought out men in the barracks who were prepared to mount a counter-attack to regain control of the fort's exterior, but as quickly as he gathered reluctant men, they slipped away. Hearing that the German pioneers were on top of Bloc I and therefore capable of dominating the entrance, he gave up the idea of a counter-attack.

Henri Lecluse was still at his post in Visé 2:

> Our casemate was fired on again, and we soon learn that Visé 1 has been knocked out. Only ours [and Cu Sud] is left. When will it be our turn? We take all of the useful precautions: the barricade of steel beams is placed at the foot of the stairwell. A light odour of chlorine can be smelled, and we are told to switch to general filters for our masks, but these only last for a few hours.
>
> I was told to come down from the upper-floor telephone chamber to the lower floor, because the Major said that the enemy were throwing charges down the gun barrels. We received a crate of grenades for the eventuality of the enemy infiltrating into the fort. We did not speak of help or the Germans being chased from the fort; we were in despair. Our premier chef descended to the barracks to see what was happening, and he did not return.

By mid-morning, there was a sense of pessimism growing in the fort, fuelled by regular detonations and fume-laden air that was

186

reaching all parts of the fort. At 1000 hours, Major Jottrand called together the fort's Defence Council in his office, where he summarised the situation, but despite the sense of resignation amongst his officers, he decided to address his men in the wide corridor of the barracks. Henri Lecluse was amongst the men waiting in the barracks:

A lot of people talked about surrender and others about a massive sortie, but this was all vague talk. In a room, a man shouted about surrender, and we were told to get out of the barracks, because the Germans had climbed down the air chimney and could drop grenades into the rooms in the central intersection. The commandant asked us if we would surrender, and seeing that a sortie would be a massacre, the majority proclaimed Yes.

Having been barracked by men who wanted to surrender, Major Jottrand returned to his office to plan the details of the surrender.

Cupola Sud

The crew of Cu Sud, who had been consistently in action, firing their guns in support of the 7th Division's attempts to retake the bridges, recorded in their report:

Alas, we received information from the Command Post that the fort was going to surrender, and the order was given to put the cupola out of service.

It was thus that, heavy-hearted, Mdlis Hanot and Fourrter who had joined us earlier as reinforcements were constrained to ask several valiant survivors of the crew for straps to create extensions to the handle of the firing lever, so as to put the building out of action.

To put the cupola out of action, it was basically a question of loading the two 75 mm guns and of setting off the firing lever from the level below to fire the pair of shells into the heart of the casemate with the cupola lowered. Not knowing what the consequences would be, Fourrter and Hanot said their potential last farewells to each other. The guns fired, the shells exploded in the tubes, and then there was silence. The last building of the fort concluded its heroic mission.

It is no exaggeration to say that the whole crew, without fail, had done their duty. Even the enemy officially recognised that Cupola Sud alone had been a casemate that they had never succeeding in attacking, due to the resistance of its valiant crew.

With the last mission accomplished, we returned to the underground barracks, and we were not wrong in considering that the whole garrison, officers at their head, seemed to wait for us before leaving the fort in surrender.

Henri Lecluse witnessed the final act of the battle:

Then came the surrender of the fort and the opening of the gates. Two captains were arguing about who would have this unpleasant duty of surrendering the fort, while others searched for a bugle and a white flag. A soldier carried an old broom with a sheet and advanced slowly down the long corridor; Captain Vamecq and a bugler sounded the surrender, but the Germans were still firing. On the second attempt, the Germans accepted the surrender without condition.

Some men were crying, while others carried cases of dynamite with which to blow up the casemates. The showers were rendered useless along with the diesel generators, except for the one lighting the hospital; we were frightened to go out, but it was with a heavy heart that we left our castle that we were so proud of, but which alas proved to be so weak.

Lecluse's opinion was that 'A clearer and stronger command would have lengthened the defence, but the ordinary soldiers

'A soldier carried an old broom with a sheet', the moment of surrender as the nervous Belgians emerged from their fortress.

Victorious *fallschirmjäger* at the end of the battle.

Witzig's men of *Sturmgruppe Granit* arrive in Maastricht.

did their duty,' while the brave men of Cu Sud, who had fought throughout the battle, had similar feelings: 'What a sad end, as our only reward lay in wait for us at the exit ... a trip to five long years of captivity'.

For the Germans, the experience of the end of the battle was different. Relief that they had survived, grief at the loss of comrades in arms, and pride in their highly significant achievement goes without saying. *Leutnant* Witzig wrote:

> *As we left the fort, after burying our dead and handing over the thirty Belgian prisoners we had captured on the upper surface to Pioneer Battalion 51, we saw scattered around the entrance installations the weapons of the garrison, which with their commander, Major Jottrand, were taken away into captivity.*

Meanwhile, on 11 May 1940 Berlin was announcing the success:

> *The High Command of the German Army makes the following announcement: the strongest fort at Liege, Eben Emael, which commands the crossings over the Maas and the Albert Canal at and to the west of Maastricht has surrendered this afternoon. The commander and 1,000 men were taken prisoner.'*

With Fort Eben Emael and the Albert Canal bridges taken, the 'Maastricht Gateway' was open, and the panzers were driving into the heart of Belgium, focusing Allied attention on this attack. Meanwhile, forty miles to the south, the German main effort was gathering momentum on the narrow roads of the Belgian Ardennes.

Honours

A success at the beginning of a campaign is to be rewarded with medals for significant military achievement, but the presentation ceremonies are also a part of the propaganda war – for both internal and external consumption. The swift capture of the world's strongest fortress by a powerful new part of the armed forces; the *fallschirmjäger* was of course of immense value to the Germans.

On 15 May 1940, an investiture was held at the *Führer* Headquarters, the *Felsennest,*

190

General *der Flieger* Student congratulating the men of *Sturmabteilung* Koch.

Adolf Hitler and the officers of *Sturmabteilung* Koch following the awarding of the Knights Cross.

near Bad Munstereifel. *Hauptmann* Koch, *Leutnant* Witzig, the officers leading the various *Sturmgruppe* and six other *fallschirmjäger*, including *Feldwebel* Wenzel, received the *Ritterkreutz* (Knights Cross), while there was a generous allowance of Iron Crosses 1st and 2nd Class for the NCOs and men of *Sturmabteilung Koch*. On 21 May 1940, *Oberleutnant* Hans Mikosch and *Oberfeldwebel* Josef Portsteffen, representing Pioneer Battalion 51, also received their decorations from the *Führer*.

Oberfeldwebel **Portseffen.**

192

Chapter 10

THE AIR ATTACKS ON THE BRIDGES

The loss of Eben Emael and the Bridges was a disaster for the Belgians, the extent of which did not take long to sink in. As the British Official History states:

> *The Belgian defence of the Albert Canal front had been gravely prejudiced by the loss of the bridges at Briedgen, Veldwezelt and Veronhoven, immediately west of Maastricht, and of the nearby frontier fortress of Eben Emael which was designed to protect them.*

Consequently, the Belgian Air Force, with their now active British and French Allies, prepared to cut off the increasingly dangerous penetration of the PFL by bombing the Meuse and Albert Canal bridges. However, as this was Sixth *Armee's* main effort, they were well covered by anti-aircraft guns and protected by combat air patrols. The Allied air operations over the bridges were destined to be extremely costly. The Official History describes the action of the British bombers of the Air Component and of the Advanced Air Striking Force, but this

The Fairey Battle bomber had a crew of three. It flew at 240 mph and carried a 1,000 lb bomb load.

description is common to all the Allied air forces: 'their sustained attacks without hesitation makes splendid but sad reading.' A telling comment from an Official History. It goes on to say,

> In conformity with prearranged plans, these medium bombers were mainly engaged in attacks against enemy columns, concentrations, and communications behind the enemy front. They soon found that such targets were strongly guarded at high level by large numbers of fighters and at low level by quick-firing anti-aircraft artillery and machine guns. Our fighter forces were not strong enough to contest successfully the enemy's air mastery over his own positions, so our bombers mostly went in to attack at low level, trusting to speed and surprise to save them from ground defence. But their speed was not great enough, and the enemy's defence was too strong to give them more than an outside chance to return unscathed, if at all, from such sorties.

Attacks on Saturday 11 May 1940

The small Belgian Air Force mounted the first air attacks on the Albert Canal bridges, including the bridge at nearby Briedgen. No less than nine of its sixteen bombers (British-made Fairey Battle aircraft) were tasked on what was considered to be a vital mission to destroy the bridges in order to restore the integrity of the Albert Canal defences. Taking off at dawn, the Battles of 5 Squadron *3eme Regiment d'Aeronautique* were over the bridges about the same time that the first panzers were arriving from Maastricht. An operations officer from 4th Panzer Division said:

> We had taken over the bridgeheads on the evening of the 10th and now the first Panzers were rolling. Panzer Regiment 35 crossed at the head of the Division the next morning and proceeded into the small bridgehead of Vroenhoven, surrounded by Belgian infantrymen. Suddenly we saw that these Belgian infantrymen were leaving their positions, forming into a column, and were about to march off to the rear. Immediately we sent out a runner from the panzer Kompanie to the Belgians and demanded that they should surrender, and we succeeded in making them turn around and they marched to us to become prisoners of war.

Under heavy fire from anti-aircraft guns, which the Germans had deployed around the bridges as a priority, three of the slow Belgian aircraft were to attack each bridge, and pressed home their attack through an inferno of fire, each armed with sixteen 50 kilo bombs. The bombs that landed in the vicinity of the bridges did little damage. Six of the nine aircraft were shot down.

At the request of the Belgians, the British and French mounted attacks later in the day on the Maastricht crossings and the German spearheads. Twenty-three RAF Bristol-Blenheim Mk-IV medium bombers of 110 Squadron were tasked to strike at the Meuse bridges during the afternoon. They succeeded in causing some damage and delay to German crossing operations, at the cost of two aircraft. 21 Squadron attacked the German spearheads that were moving on the road from Vroenhoven (Objective *Beton*) towards the south east. They had far less flack to contend with, but although the amount of

Bristol Blenheim aircraft, like other British bombers, was found to be obsolescent in the face of German anti-aircraft fire.

Maastricht and the blown bridges. Bombs can be seen detonating in the river just south of the bridges.

damage they inflicted is unknown, the German advance was not checked for long.

Over the Maastricht target at 1830 hours, thirteen French LeO 45 aircraft repeated the attack on the German crossing site. This time, the Germans were fully prepared, and the French aircrew of 12eme Squadron received a hot reception, reporting that they 'flew into sheets of fire arcing up from the city'. It is recorded that three French aircraft were lost in the target area; even after a night of hard work by the French ground crews, only one of the ten remaining that limped home, riddled with holes, was deemed airworthy.

139 Squadron badge.

Above: German 20 mm anti-aircraft gun at the Veldwezelt bridge. Below: A 40 mm gun.

Attacks on Sunday 12 May 1940

Following the casualties suffered the day before, over the heavily defended Maastricht Gateway, Air Marshal Barratt ordered that the crews of the British aircraft that were to mount the renewed attack should all be volunteers. In the case of No. I Group's 12 Squadron, volunteers for this vital mission were called for 'and the whole squadron stepped forward'. In this case, six crews were nominated, on the grounds that they were already at the head of the duty roster. However, ahead of them were the volunteers of another squadron.

Flying from Plivot in France before dawn, nine Blenheim aircraft of 139 Squadron were to attack German troops moving on an axis southeast from the Albert Canal shortly after first light. Approaching under the cover of dark, the aircraft successfully dive-bombed the German column with their 1,000-pound bomb loads, but as they started to head home, enemy fighters fell on them. Only two aircraft returned to Plivot, and another two were seen going down in flames. A pair of airmen from an aircraft that came down near the Belgian lines subsequently rejoined the squadron. The remaining crews were either killed or taken prisoner of war.

Next to attack the area were the six Battles of No. 12 Squadron, known as the 'Shiny Twelve' or, unofficially, the 'Dirty Dozen'. However, one aircraft found that its bomb-release mechanism was jammed, and did not join the attack that was delivered at about 0900 hours. The Official History states that:

... in the end only five [Battles] *were actually employed; for cover they were given two squadrons of fighters* [one of which were hurricanes of No. 1 Squadron] *from the Air Component and ten Hurricanes from the Advanced Air Striking Force. But these were, of course, no protection from ground defences.*

Panzers streaming across the Vroenhoven Bridge.

No. 12 Squadron's targets were the Albert Canal bridges at Vroenhoven and Veldwezelt; three aircraft were allocated to each bridge. The pilot, Flying Officer Donald Garland, a 21-year-old Irishman, navigator Sergeant Thomas Gray, who was a pre-war regular airman, and Leading Air Crewman Lawrence Reynolds, the rear gunner, led the attack on the Veldwezelt Bridge. Flying Officer Norman Thomas led the aircraft into the attack on the Vroenhoven Bridge.

Both bridges were defended by very heavy anti-aircraft artillery; some sources suggest that 300 guns and machine guns were in the area of the Albert Canal and Meuse Bridges; and some reports suggest that there were over 100 Messerschmitt BF109's in action. All of the British aircraft were damaged or destroyed by the AA batteries. However, the five Battles duly flew into the attack, in what for the aircrews was their first operational bombing raid.

Flying Officer Thomas dived down to the Vroenhoven Bridge and hit one end of the structure with one of his bombs, but his aircraft was badly hit and he made a forced landing. Thomas and his crew all survived the crash, but were captured by German troops. Pilot Officer Thomas Davy, following in on the attack, bombed short of the target and was hit in the wing: ordering his crew to bail out, he struggled to save his burning aircraft, but crash-landed a few miles from their airfield. The aircraft was written off,

12 Squadron badge.

but Davy survived the crash landing, and his crew who had bailed out were captured. On 31 May 1940, Pilot Officer Thomas Davy was informed that he had been awarded the Distinguished Flying Cross for his part in the action earlier in the month.

Shortly after the attack on the Vroenhoven Bridge had begun, Flying Officer Garland led his three Battles into the attack on the Veldwezelt Bridge. Having released their bombs over the target, Flying Officer Garland and his crew died when their Battle crashed near the village of Lanaken, three miles to the north of the bridge. After the raid, Belgian civilians recovered the bodies and secretly buried them, to prevent the Germans taking them; after the liberation in late 1944, an Allied grave registration unit was notified of the location and the three airmen were re-interred in the Lanaken cemetery; after the war, the bodies were moved to the Commonwealth War Graves Commission cemetery at Haverlee, near Louvain.

The second Battle, flown by Pilot Officer McIntosh, was hit in the fuel tanks on the run-in to target, setting the aircraft on fire. McIntosh jettisoned his bombs and made a forced landing; the crew survived as prisoners of war. The third Battle piloted by Sergeant Fred Marland released its bombs, but then, raked by anti-aircraft fire, went into an uncontrolled dive into the ground, killing all the crew.

Aerial photography confirmed that the western end of the Veldwezelt Bridge was badly damaged, probably by the attacks by Garland and Gray. Damage on the Vroenhoven Bridge appeared to be less serious. According to the British Official History,

The German War Diary of XVI Corps records that on May the 12th the Maastricht bridges and the marching columns of the 4th Panzer Division "are separately attacked by enemy bombers. Considerable delays result from this." General Guderian's XIX Corps War Diary notes on the 12th that "Enemy fighter activity is exceptionally vigorous; in the evening the enemy carried out repeated air attacks against the crossing-points and in doing so sustained heavy casualties."

Following heavy casualties, the slow-flying Battles of 12 Squadron were withdrawn, clearly obsolescent in comparison with the newer and more capable German opponents and anti-aircraft systems. The Battle took part in night operations for some time, before finding a role as a training aircraft.

Later on 12 May, French bombers carried out attacks on the same targets, but also suffered terribly from concentrated German flak; and in another disastrous raid, on 14 May 1940, No. 12 Squadron lost another five out of six aircraft.

The Victoria Cross

The pilot and navigator of the aircraft that led the attack on the Albert Canal bridges, Flying Officer Garland, and Sergeant Gray, who was educated at Warminster Secondary School, Wiltshire, were both posthumously awarded the Victoria Cross, Britain's highest award for bravery, and the first to be given during the Second World War. It was unusual for two members of the crew to receive the Victoria Cross, and LAC Reynolds apparently did not receive the award, as he was deemed not to have been in a position to influence the decision to press home the attack. Their medal citation published in the *London Gazette* on 11 June 1940 reads:

Flying Officer Garland VC.

Flying Officer Garland was the Pilot and Sergeant Gray was the Observer of the leading aircraft of a formation of 5 aircraft that attacked a bridge over the Albert Canal, which had not been destroyed and was allowing the enemy to advance into Belgium. All the aircrews of the Squadron concerned volunteered for the operation and, after five crews had been selected by drawing lots, the attack was delivered at low altitude against this vital target. Orders were issued that this bridge was to be destroyed at all costs. As had been expected, exceptionally intense machine gun and anti-aircraft fire were encountered. Moreover, the bridge area was heavily protected by enemy fighters. In spite of this, the formation successfully delivered a dive-bombing attack from the lowest practicable altitude. British fighters in the vicinity reported that the target was obscured by the bombs bursting on it and near it. Only one of the five aircraft returned from this mission. The pilot of this aircraft reported that besides being subject to extremely heavy anti-aircraft fire, through which they dived to attack the objective, our aircraft were also attacked by a large number of enemy fighters after they had released their bombs on the target. Much of the success of this vital operation must

Sergeant Gray VC.

be attributed to the Formation Leader, Flying Officer Garland, and to the coolness and resource of Sergeant Gray, who in the most difficult conditions navigated Flying Officer Garland's aircraft in such a manner that the whole formation was able successfully to attack the target in spite of subsequent heavy losses. Flying Officer Garland and Sergeant Gray did not return.

Tour of the Fort and Bridges

A visit to Fort Eben Emael and the surrounding 10 May 1940 battle area is extreme worthwhile and will take up most of a day. To fully appreciate the significance of Eb. Emael's place in Belgium's 1940 defensive plans, visitors should first take a look at the Albert Canal and later ensure that they visit Bloc 01 on the fort's upper surface, where the tactical importance of the fort can be fully appreciated.

While approaching Eben Emael, keep a look out for a wooded conical hill and near industrial chimney. This landmark is St Peter's Hill on the Dutch side of the Albert Cana Fort Eben Emael is a short way to the south.

To reach the fort from the west take Junction 32 off the E313/A13 onto the N79 toward Maastricht. On reaching Riemst turn right, taking the N671. Alternatively, continue on the N79 (3 miles) to the Vroenhoven Bridge to view the Albert Canal.

From the east i.e. the Maastricht ring road, take the N79 signed for Tongeren. Cross the Albert Canal at Vroenhoven and in Riemst, turn left onto the N671.

Follow the Eben Emael road signs onto the N619 at the roundabout. Drive through the village of Eben to Eben Emael. Pass the church and look out for signs to the fort on the right (Rue du Garage) and park.

Tour of the Fort

The fort, the upper surface and the ground alongside, remains the property of the Belgia Army who, for many years, used it for a variety of training functions but since 1998 the for has been administered by the 'Association Fort Eben Emael' (asbl). However, the Belgia Defence Ministry is now actively maintaining exterior parts of the fort as a militar monument.

The fort is regularly open at weekends to the public, monthly from March to November During these weekends, visitors can both enter the fort and explore the superstructure Details of public open days, hours and entry fees can be found a 'http://www.fort-eben-emael.be'. There is normally a tour in English around mid-day bu contacting the fort is recommended. Booking visits to Eben Emael at other times can be made (see website for details), however, this facility is normally only available to groups o larger private tours.

For obvious safety reasons, tours of the fort's labyrinthine galleries are conducted by volunteer Belgian guides. However, the order in which the fort's internal features are described in Chapter 2 is approximately in line with the normal tour route, although, as access to additional areas of the fort is opened, the route taken is becoming more variable. It is worth following progress underground by using the map on page 34. Please note the following advice, issued by the asbl:

- It is not possible to visit the whole fort.
- A visit to the interior of Cupola 120 can NOT be guaranteed.
- A visit to the Command Posts complex is an alternative to CU 120.
- The tour in the interior of the fort covers just under a mile.
- Visitors with heart problems or other health considerations, should think twice before considering a visit to the upper galleries! The tour involves climbing several long staircases. However, a visit to the barracks is confined to the lower level and is safe for most.
- Those who suffer from claustrophobia are also not encouraged to visit the upper galleries.

The Guardroom Bloc I.

● The temperature in the fort is approximately 11 degrees Celsius, therefore visitors should always wear warm clothes and comfortable shoes.

● Remember, the fort was built for the military, not for civilians: for the safety of the group and yourself follow the guide's instructions at all times during your visit.

● Smoking is not allowed in the galleries of the fort.

● Mobile telephones do not work inside the fort.

● Do not leave the group 'to wander': you could end up being confined in the fort in total darkness!

● Do not take items from the fort: as military property, the fort is within the jurisdiction of the Belgian military police!

tour of the fort, including a stop in the Café, the fort's ~rmer kitchen, normally takes 2-3 hours and normally ~cludes:

Machine gun mount, Bloc I.

● The machinery-room (generators)
● The Commander's office
● The guardroom cell (signed 'Cachots' or Cells)
● The officers' mess
● The infirmary
● Officers, SNCOs and soldiers barrack room
● The ventilation system
● A display with German uniforms
● The room of remembrance
● V1 display
● The ablutions

Tour of the Upper Surface

The tour of the fort's interior gives the visitor a particularly strong Belgian perspective of what it was like to live and fight in Eben Emael during early May 1940. To complete the story, a visit to the upper surface is a must. From here the problems facing *Leutnant* Witzig and his *fallschirmjäger* can be fully appreciated along with the dramatic views from Bloc 01 to the east, which demonstrate the fort's pivotal role in the defence of this part of Belgium. The major difference between 1940 and today is that there are many more trees and bushes on the slopes and in the moat surrounding much of the fort. The hanger building on the upper surface has gone and the football field is now used for growing crops.

Public visits to the upper surface are normally only possible on public visit days. Groups on other occasions are able to visit the upper surface if they have permission from the Belgian Military authorities via the asbl.

The ahst have issued the following advice and warnings:

● The trail is across country. It is steep, there are tripping hazards and it can be muddy, wet and slippery. Please wear appropriate footwear/clothing and take care as you walk.

● Remain on the footpaths.

● Be aware that the upper surface has been used for military training and nothing

The view across Holland from Bloc OI east.

The Bloc II bell shaowing the effect of a hollow charge.

should be picked up or touched

● Adhere to any instructions given by ab guides or the Belgian military.

1. The trail starts to the left or behind Blc 1. Note the single surviving dummy 120 mr cupola on display in this area. Once on the upper surface, follow the numbered rout (wooden posts) maps of the current route ar available from the shop. Be aware that the route to the upper surface can be muddy an slippery.

2. Visé 2. Not attacked as it faced soutl towards Visé, not north towards the Alber Canal bridges. Nor could it fire caniste rounds onto the upper surface which woulc have threatened the *fallschirmjäger*.

3. Chimney. This is the armoured chimney through which foul air and generator fumes were vented.

4. Maastricht 2/ Eben III OP. Taken in the first part of the assault by *Feldwebe* Niedermeir's 1 Section. Note the large steel OP cupola. See page 106 for details.

4 bis. Cu 120. Follow the path across the field to the concrete casemate. Note that the modern replacement barrel covers are somewhat larger than the originals that were blown off by the explosion of the hollow charges. One of the barrels is elevated. See page 140 for details.

Cupola Sud. This casemate is not on the official tour but from the track to Point 5, it can be seen to the right. Unlike Cu Nord, it is frozen in the elevated position and is therefore worth the effort to visit.

5. Anti-tank Moat. Even though this track is surrounded by trees, it is easy to appreciate the depth of the moat and the steepness of the defences on the southern flank. The crossing was built over the moat after the war.

Bloc IV. This good view of Bloc IV shows one of the smaller crew observation bells located on the defensive Blocs.

7 via 6. Bloc 01. Follow the track to the right to reach the observation post at Bloc 01. Be aware that there is a 150 foot drop to the canal path below and that there are no fences. Take care. The asbl recommend that visitors:

● Keep a safe distance from the edge of the Bloc, especially in wet weather conditions.

● Do not go beyond the cupola. Beware of the drop.

● Children should not be left unattended under any circumstances.

● Do not climb around the Bloc or venture onto steep ground.

9 via 8. Cupola Nord. At the time of writing the asbl have restored the traversing mechanism to a working condition and the Belgian military are repairing the concrete. See page 99 for details of Feldwebel Unger's attack.

10. Visé 1. The glider carrying the section who were to neutralise this casemate did not arrive and it was therefore taken by one of the reserve sections. See page 124 for the story.

12 via 11. Mi Nord. This was Witzig and Wenzel's HQ. Its capture is described starting page 116.

13. Mi Sud. Heavily damaged, this casemate and Mi Nord were originally surrounded barbed wire. See page 114.

The path to Ma 1 and Bloc 2 is across the track and down through the woods. This track very steep in places, especially in its lower section and can be extremely slippery. If in doubt, take the easier route down via the chimney and Bloc I by following the edge of the wood.

14. Maastricht 1. *Feldwebel* Peter Arent's capture of the casemate is described at page 110 and the story of his destruction of the stairway the following morning is at page 47.

15. Bloc 2. The attack by *Feldwebel* Arent and *Oberfeldwebel* Portseffen was restaged several days after the real event and filmed by the German propaganda Ministry .

Follow the made-up track back to the car park in front of Bloc I.

The Bridges.

time allows it is worth visiting both the Albert Canal and Maastricht bridges. However, the latter are in the centre of a modern city and consequently suffer all the associated disadvantages of traffic and parking. As already noted, Maastricht is a good place to find larger hotels within walking distance of the bridges.

This tour is written with the independent visitor, who is travelling in a light vehicle, in mind. Those with larger vehicles, such as the bigger mini buses and definitely coaches will have to adapt the route and expect to have to walk further from roads and parking appropriate to their size and weight.

The asbl are currently negotiating a cycle way from the fort to the points described below. If driving, please watch out for cyclists and avoid obstructing cycle paths; it is illegal and causes great offence.

2nd Grenadiers' memorial at Kanne.

The Albert Canal Bridges.

From the fort's car park, take the route back to the main road through village of Eben Emael and turn right.Follow the road from Emael to Opkanne, on the western bank of the canal. There are many more houses than in 1940 but the topography is unchanged.

Kanne Bridge (Objective *Eisen*).

The original angular girder bridge, successfully blown by the 2nd Grenadiers, has been replaced by a bow girder structure, which at the time of writing is itself being replaced. Turn off before going over the bridge and take the concrete surfaced road up the hill. Where the road opens out at a bend park and take the track marked Tienderberg and 'Engls-Canadees herdenkingsmonument'. Two hundred yards up this track, you will see a stone memorial on top of a Belgian 1940 pillbox built into the side of the hill overlooking the bridge. This is the memorial to the 2nd Grenadiers who held this sector of the canal line and blew the bridge.

Oberfeldwebel **Portsteffen's Crossing Point**. In order to reach Portsteffen's crossing point, having crossed the bridge and entered the village, take the first right. Drive past the school and church and turn right at the T-junction. Follow the road through the houses and out onto a rough road running above and parallel with the canal. Park at the junction with Silexweg and walk down to the canal. Walk towards St Pierres' Hill where the canal enters the cutting. It should be noted that the canal was widened after the war and the point where *Oberfeldwebel* Portsteffen crossed the canal has been further widened to provide berths for barges Note that Bloc Canal Sud was removed when the canal was widened. Retrace the route back in to Kanne turning left into Brusraat and right before the no entry sign. Turn right and then fork left following sign to Vroenhoven.

Vroenhoven Bridge (Objective *Beton*). On reaching the N79, turn left, cross the bridge and turn right immediately and park behind the concrete bunker. The two memorials are to the defenders of the bridge and opposite to those of the whole of the 18th Infantry Regiment. Walking back onto the original bridge, it is easy to appreciate the significance of the Albert Canal as a strategic obstacle that was expected to delay the enemy for five days.

Maastricht Cemetery. Re-cross the bridge heading east towards Maastricht on the N79. The cemetery is just over a mile on the left. Park opposite the main entrance. The British and Belgian graves are 150 yards on the right. The British graves are mainly aircrew, with a number of June 1940 Army graves belonging to prisoners of war who died of their wounds on the way back to PoW camps. Of the aircrew, most are bomber crews from later in the war, including a whole Canadian crew. However, there are graves of men killed in the May 1940 air attacks of the Albert Canal bridges.

Veldwezelt Bridge (Objective *Stahl*). Retrace the route to the Vroenhoven Bridge and continue west on the N79 and turn right on the N78 to Veldwezelt. On reaching the outskirts of Veldwezelt turn right onto the N2, signed towards Maasik. Cross the bridge and park. To the right is a small brick and marble memorial to the airmen of 12 Squadron. Flying Officer Garland VC and Sergeant Gray VC are buried at Heverlee CWGC Cemetery near Leuven, east of Brussels.

Re-crossing the bridge, turn right towards the centre of Veldwezelt. After half a mile there is a civilian cemetery on the left. The cemetery contains the graves of Belgians belonging to the Regiments that defended the Albert Canal line. There is also a group of simple white crosses, which are the graves of Belgian civilians killed by enemy action.

Continue east to Maastricht on the N2.

The Maastricht Bridges. Maastricht has expanded greatly since the war, particularly west to the Albert Canal and it is an illuminating exercise to compare a contemporary map. There were three bridges across the River Meuse/Maas in Maastricht in 1940. From south to north, the first was a narrow bridge that was little more than a crossing for pedestrians or bicycles. In the middle was the main road bridge, which was the Germans' primary objective. The third bridge was a railway bridge a thousand yards to the north. The two dual carriageway bridges that carry the ring road are modern additions.

The bridges are easy to find, however, parking is not. An evening visit is recommended.

Section blown by the Dutch.

Eben Emael ———

Maas/Meuse River

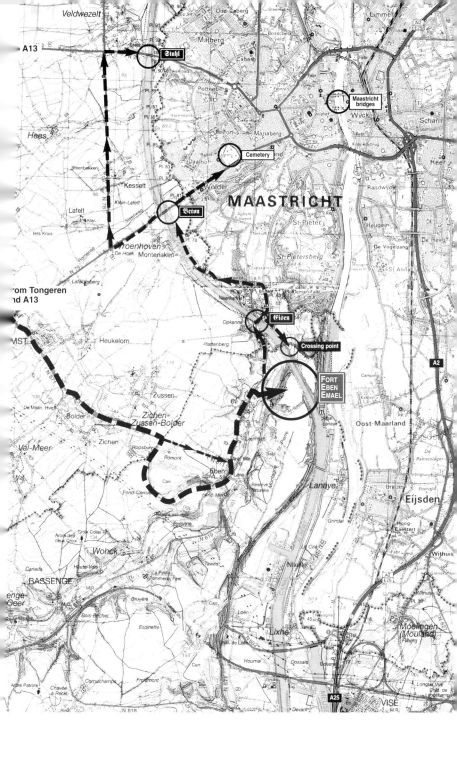

Airborne Forces (German) 55-58
Albert canal 7, 17, 19-21, 27, 30, 51-54, 63, 70, 77,
    80, 92, 96, 97, 120, 131, 132, 135, 138, 145, 153,
    157-171, 175, 176,181, 190, 193-201
Ardennes 7, 63, 70, 72
Belgian Army Formations:
    I Army Corps 42, 43
    7th Division 43, 131, 132, 138, 140, 159, 167, 186, 187
    Position Fortifee de Liege (PFL) 14, 19, 42, 96,
    131, 135, 138, 146, 150, 152, 186, 193
    Regiment Fortifee de Liege 16, 25, 27, 43, 15
    2nd Grenadier Regiment 42, 138, 146, 168-169
    2nd Rifle Regiment 42, 164-166
    18th Infantry Regiment 42, 160, 164
    Fort Eben Emael
        Administrative Group 23-24
        1st Battery 23, 41
        2nd Battery 23, 41
Belgian neutrality & strategy 12-13, 15, 16
Blitzkrieg 55, 63, 68-69, 153
Brilmont, General Henri-Alexis 9, 10, 11, 12
Castert, Tranchee de 19, 21, 23, 30, 127
Cremer, Sergant 123-124, 129-131, 140-145
DFS 230 Glider 58-63, 74, 78, 80, 85-92, 96-101,
    103-104, 114, 136, 159, 160, 164-165, 168
Eben Emael
    Alert, sounding of the 93-96
    Arc of fire 23
    Decision to build, construction & cost   19, 21
    Garrison 23-27
    Morale 25-27
    Strength & under manning 23-25
    Surrender 39, 188-190
    External barrack buildings 27, 37, 93, 114
    Fake Cupolas 51, 115, 116, 121
    Lower Level 22, 29-41
    Ablutions & armourer's workshop 35
    Barracks internal 39
    Cells & generators 36
    Commander's Office 37
    Infirmary 39-40
    Intermediate Level 22,41-44, 109, 127
    Command Post 42, 125, 127, 129, 146, 147, 151, 187
    Ammunition magazines 43-44
    Upper Level 22, 27, 45-51, 121, 127
    AA Machine Guns 21, 49-50, 102, 103-106, 127
    Bloc I (Entrance) 27, 28-29, 33-35, 41, 97, 127, 138, 185, 186
    Bloc II 27, 29, 127, 183, 185
    Bloc Canal Nord 30, 180, 181, 186
    Bloc Canal Sud 30
    Bloc 01 30
    Bloc IV 31, 106
    Bloc V 32, 103, 131, 145, 151
    Bloc VI 23, 181, 183, 186
    Cupola-120 43, 49, 99, 106, 121-124, 127, 128-131, 134,
        140-145
    Cupola Nord 47-49, 94, 99-103, 104, 105, 123, 127, 128,
        131, 132, 151
    Cupola Sud 47-49, 95, 127, 131-132, 145, 186, 187-188
    Ma 1 42, 45, 110-114, 147-150, 151
    Ma 2 42, 45, 106-110, 151
    Mi Nord 27,49, 94, 101, 114, 116-121, 127, 137, 150
    Mi Sud 27, 49, 94, 113-116, 150
    OPs 23, 31, 41, 46, 96, 106, 107, 117, 136
    Vi 1 42, 45, 124-127, 145-147, 149, 186
    Vi 2 42, 45, 132-135, 145-147, 150, 152, 180, 186
    Workshop hanger 51, 101-102, 127

Garland VC, Flying Officer 199-201
German Army
    Army Group A 70-72
    Army Group B 70-72
    Army Group C 70-71
    Sixth Armie 153-154, 165, 176, 193
    XXVII Korps 153, 171
    4th Panzer Division 80, 137, 153, 156, 158, 168, 1
        194
    7th Flieger Division 55-58, 77
    1st Fallschrimjager Regiment 77
    151st Infantry Regiment 80, 167, 168, 172-180, 19
    Brau-Lehr Battalion 63
    100 Zur Besonderen Verwerdung (ZBV)   153, 156
    51st Pioneer Battalion 80, 172, 177, 180, 181, 185,
    Sturmabteilung Koch 77-82, 84, 85, 86, 93, 96, 153,
    Sturmgruppe Beton 79, 121, 160-164, 173
    Sturmgruppe Eisen 79, 145, 168-171, 182
    Sturmgruppe Granit 79, 82, 87, 97, 116, 125, 128, 13
        168, 180, 181
    Plan 79-80
    Training 80-84
    Sturmgruppe Stahl 79, 89, 164-168, 173
    Glider – see DFS 230 Glider
Goering, Reichsmarshall Herman 7, 57, 58, 72
Gray VC Sergeant 200-201
Hitler, Adolf 7, 55, 68, 72-76, 82, 85, 153, 192
Hollow Charge 74-77, 99, 102-103, 104, 107-108, 111
    117-119, 125, 136, 185
Jottrand, Major Jean 24, 37-38, 42, 54, 93, 94, 97, 10
    127-128, 138, 140, 180, 187, 190
Junkers (Ju)- 87 (Stuka) 110, 121, 125, 136, 140, 144
    147, 154, 161, 163, 165, 167, 182
Junkers (Ju)-52 57, 58-61, 87-92, 96-97, 137, 159, 16
Kanne and Bridge (Eisen) 23, 30, 53, 79, 93, 97, 152,
    171, 177-180, 181, 182, 186
Koch, Hauptmann 77-79, 84, 86, 120-121, 137, 158, 1
    168, 171, 190
Lanaye Locks 30-31, 93, 97
Lange, Pilot Heiner 78, 87, 103-106, 127-128, 140
Lecluse, Henri 94, 95, 132-135, 150-152, 181, 186, 18
Liege defences 10, 11, 12, 13, 15-18, 19, 43
Longdoz, Adjutant 98, 114, 127, 129
Luftwaffe 55, 57, 80, 82, 85-92
Maas/Meuse river 8, 16, 19, 21, 53, 63, 70, 72, 80, 97,
    153, 156-157, 164, 171-176, 193
Maastricht Gateway 7, 176, 190, 196
Masstricht 17, 19, 23, 42, 53, 79, 80, 91, 94, 96, 114, 1
    154-155, 156-157, 160, 163, 171, 190
Maginot Line 15, 67, 70
Mikosch, Oberstleutnant Hans 179, 181, 182, 192
Plan (German) 72-77
Portstefen, Feldwebel Josef 180, 182, 185, 192
Special Forces (German) 63-66
St Peter's Hill (Castert Heights) 19, 20, 21, 23
Strategy in the west (German) 7, 67-72
Student, General der Flieger Kurt 55, 72-77, 90
Veldwezelt bridge 53, 79, 164-168, 182, 193, 198-201
Vise gap 11, 17, 21, 23, 31, 42, 54
Vroenhoven Bridge 23, 53, 79, 121 159, 160-164, 168, '
    193, 195, 198-201
Wenzel Oberfeldwebel 82, 89, 91-92, 98, 117-121, 127,
    137, 140, 192
Witzig Oberstleutnant Rudolf 77, 78, 79, 82, 84, 87, 88-9
    98, 120, 136-138, 147, 152, 158, 159, 177, 180, 185-1
    190, 192